Imagery From Beyond™

Book 2

a
Messages From Beyond®
Coloring Book
Featuring Art by Ali™

Alice Best Jackson & Dennis Jackson

Imagery From Beyond™ Book 2
a Messages From Beyond® Coloring Book
featuring Art by Ali™
By: Alice Best Jackson and Dennis Jackson
Copyright © 2016 Alice Best Jackson and Dennis Jackson
Lake Stevens, WA   USA
Messages From Beyond®

All Art by Ali™ designs are hand-drawn originals by Alice Best Jackson.
©Alice Best Jackson, all rights reserved.

Book concept and design by Alice Best Jackson and Dennis Jackson.
Cover borders colored by: Anabela C. Stewart (front); Karen Eggleston (back)
Back cover colored images by team colorists (left to right):
(1)Susan Brown, (2)Karen Eggleston, (3)Karen Eggleston, (4)Dennis Jackson,
(5)Dennis Jackson with border by Anabela C. Stewart,
(6)Ma. Hilda P. Lumibao, (7)Jennifer "MsRed" Scarabin, (8)Shiela Zamora

Messages From Beyond® is a U.S. trademark, registered and owned by
Dennis A. Jackson and Alice Best Jackson.

ISBN-13: 978-1532710131
ISBN-10:   1532710135

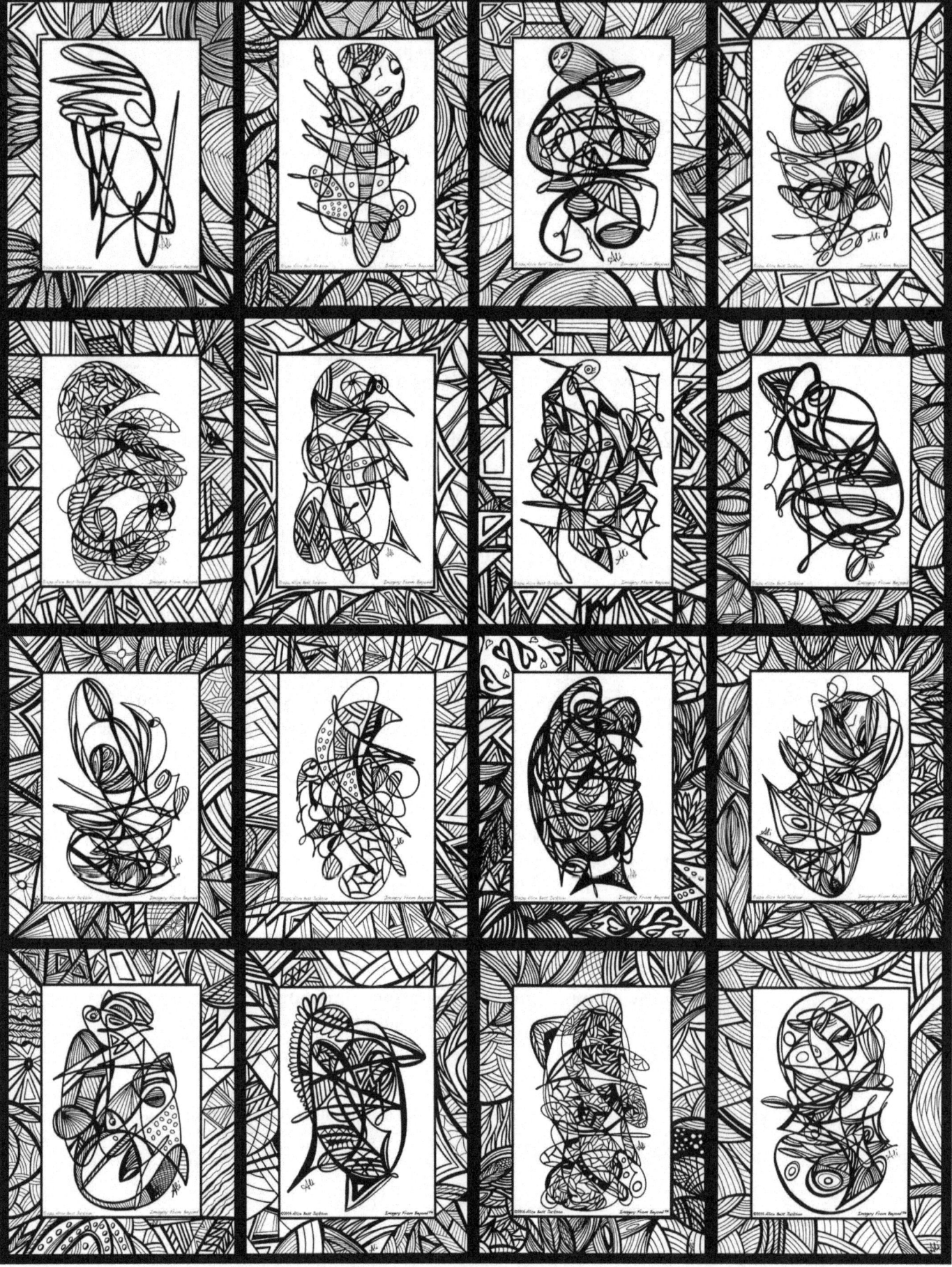

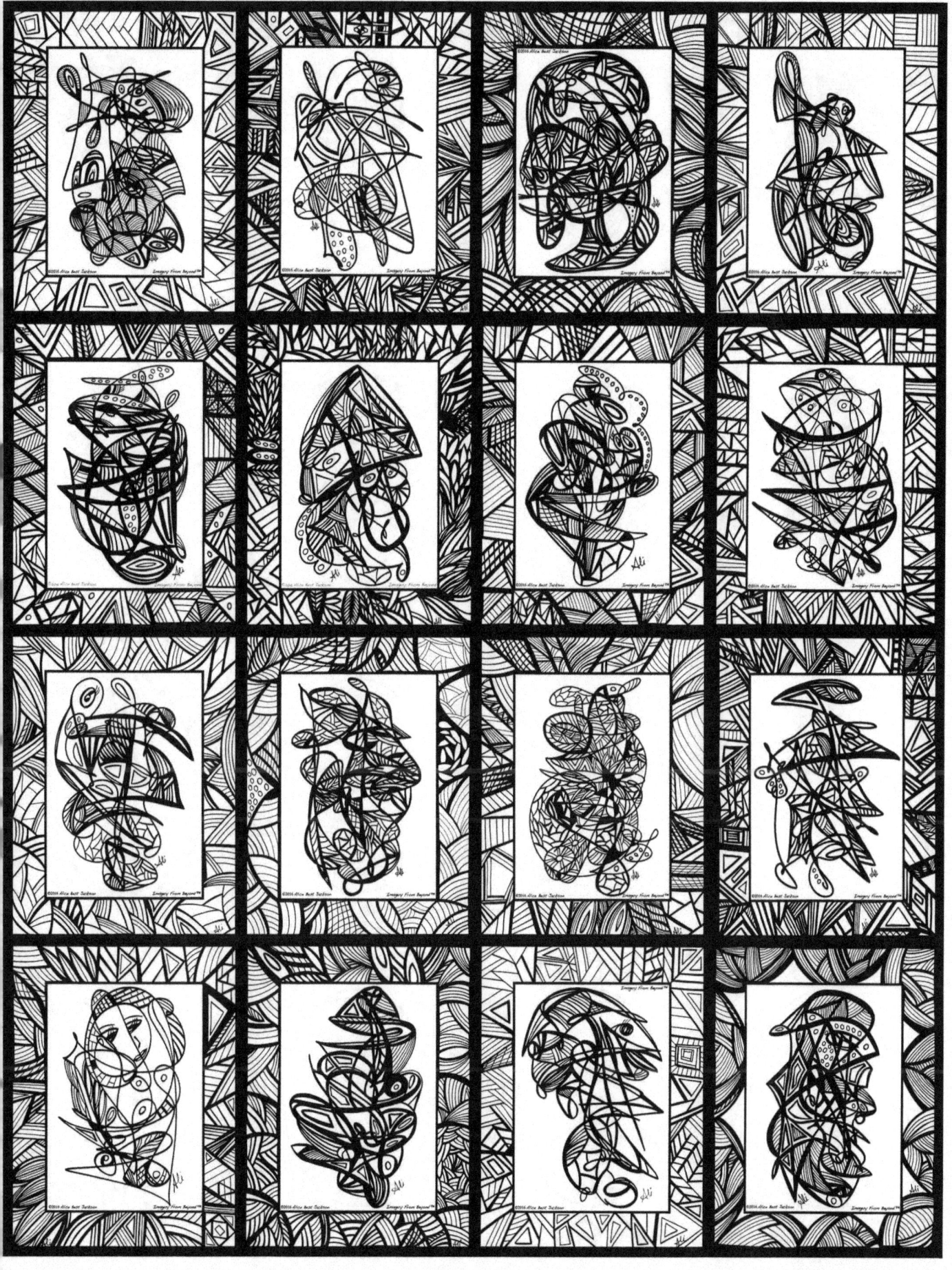

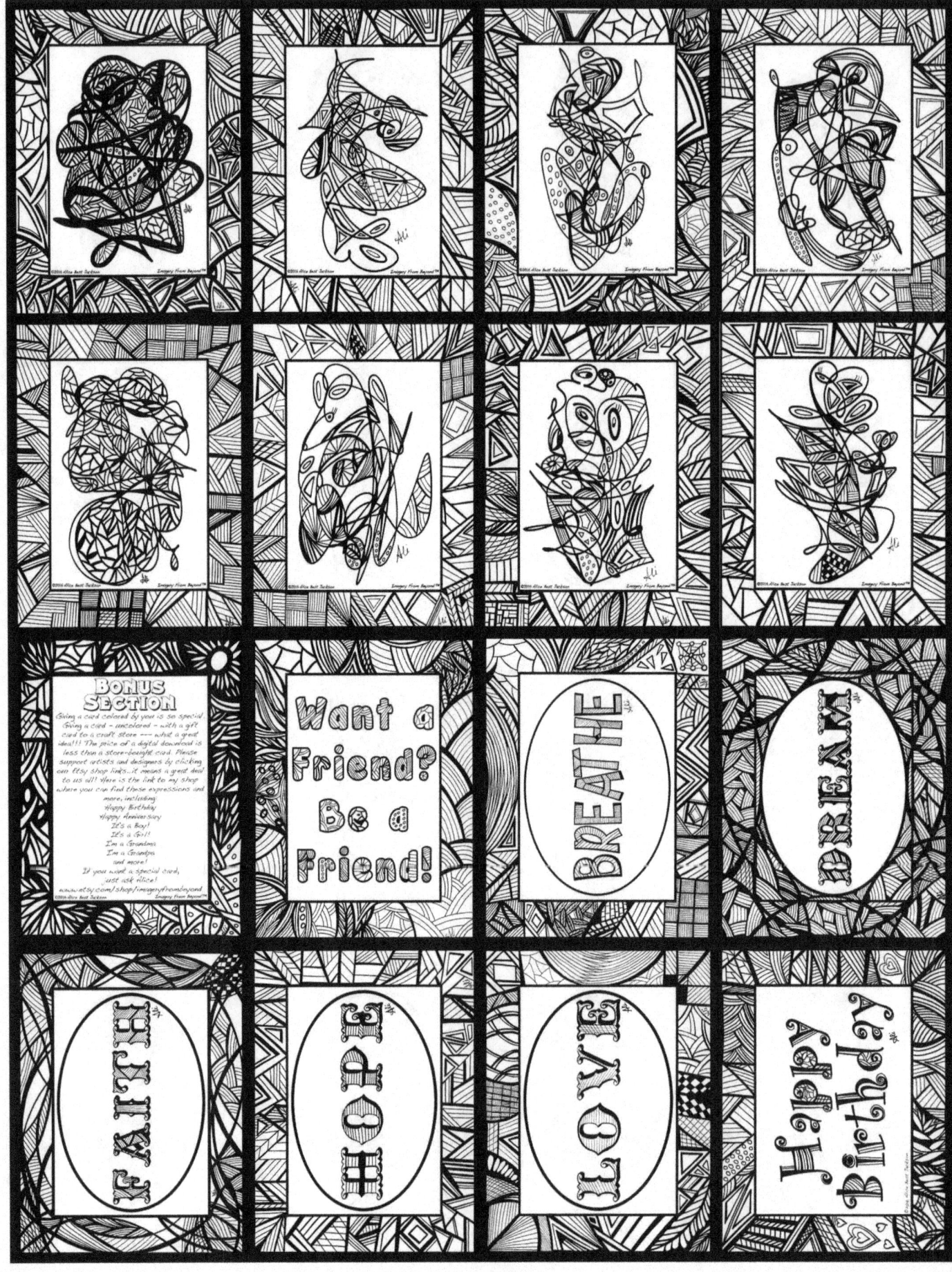

Dedicated with gratitude and appreciation
to all the colorists, artists, and
social media groups who have welcomed
us into your wonderful world of
color, talent and imagination.
You continue to inspire and encourage us.

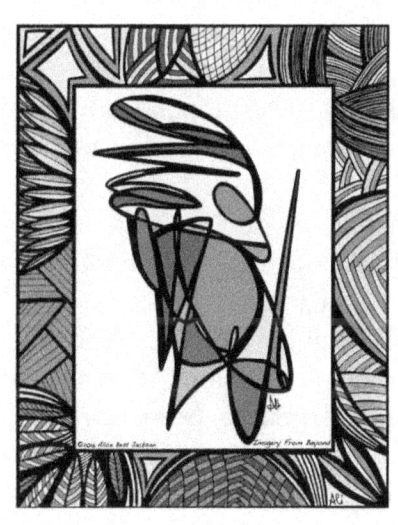

With gratitude, we acknowledge...

Behind every author and illustrator there is a village of people who encourage and cheer as each piece of the puzzle falls into place. We are blessed to have such a village, and honor each of you here and now. Our gratitude and appreciation go to friends who listened to our ramblings, offering enhanced tweaks, "oohed and aaahed" at each drawing, and eagerly encouraged us to move forward with our vision of a coloring book series.

For the second book in our *Imagery From Beyond™* series, we specifically give our heartfelt thanks to:

David Rabinowitz (1913-2001), Alice's father and mentor, an abstract artist who greatly influenced her throughout her first 50 years, and whose assistance from beyond is evident in all *Art by Ali™*;

Writers Cooperative of the Pacific Northwest (WCPNW), for your wit, wisdom, friendship, and generous sharing of information;

Coloring Book Author Support Group on Facebook, without whose daily support, ideas, and encouragement, this book would still be but a dream—many of you have become friends in every sense of the word, and we thank and honor you; and

Our many fans and friends who have supported *Messages From Beyond®* since 1997, and who received special messages along with their personal *Art by Ali™*.

We give special thanks to our phenomenal talented team of colorists across the world, whose artistic coloring is shared with many thousands of coloring fans via the Internet. For this book cover, we appreciate and gratefully honor:
Susan Brown (Washington), **Anabela C. Stewart** (New Mexico),
Jennifer "MsRed" Scarabin (Mississippi), **Karen Eggleston** (Michigan),
Shiela Zamora (Philippines), and **Ma. Hilda P. Lumibao**, (from the Philippines, but currently living in Dubai).
Your brilliant coloring skills bring life to these designs, and your gracious online sharing brings
Imagery From Beyond™ to more people than we can even imagine.

As always, hugs and love to our amazing grandchildren, Parker Best and Kennedy Best, who keep us laughing and remind us how important it is to just play!

And, of course, we thank YOU for choosing our coloring book, and for taking time from your busy life to relax and just color! Imagine the possibilities your imagination will create!

Thank you all!!
Alice and Dennis

Welcome to our world of Imagery,
featuring Intuitive Abstract Art by Ali™.

Imagination contains images. Images are within the pages of this book.
What do you see? What does each image say to you?

The drawings featured in our **Messages From Beyond® Coloring Book** series are all hand-drawn originals created specifically to help you get in touch with your innate intuitive ability. The abstract designs will allow your imagination and creativity to flow. We call our series **Imagery From Beyond™** because **Art by Ali™** is a unique style of drawing that seems to flow from Alice's pens as she creates each page. To some people, this is just a coloring book—a fun way to relieve stress and relax after a hectic day. To many others, this may become a meditation tool to promote healing as well as to facilitate communication with loved ones who are sending you messages.

As you flip through the pages, you may be drawn to a specific image...that is the place to start. The designs and even the colors you select will hold a special meaning for you. Each design magically comes to life as color is applied, and depending on the colorist's view and direction the page is turned, the images can be quite different. Let your imagination and creativity soar as you color and create your own images within these pages. There is no right or wrong way to view the page—you may turn the book any way you desire—great for left-handed colorists. The possibilities are endless—many people color the same design more than once, each time coming up with different patterns, images, and emotions. Use 1, 2, or many colors to bring the designs to life. You will begin to see various images while creating a piece of art that speaks directly to you.

Pages are purposely sized for easy framing—even the borders alone are perfect for 8x10 photo frames. For best results, the preferred tools for coloring are colored pencils, crayons, gel pens, and fine or ultra-fine-point markers. If using markers, we suggest placing a protective page behind the drawing you're coloring to prevent bleed-through colors. There are bordered sheets at the end of this book to test your colors or use as a protective blotter page, or you can color and use as a photo frame!
Please note: the artist has no control over the quality of the paper.
This is a book published on demand by CreateSpace and Amazon,
and the paper used is the best thickness available.

Many people have told us, when coloring the images, they are taken to a place where healing can begin. The therapeutic benefits of coloring, along with the personal meaning you assign to your finished pages, may bring you healing and comfort as well.
Thank you for choosing our book to be a part of your creative process.

Are you ready to get in touch with your inner child?
May peace be with you always...all ways!
Dennis and Alice

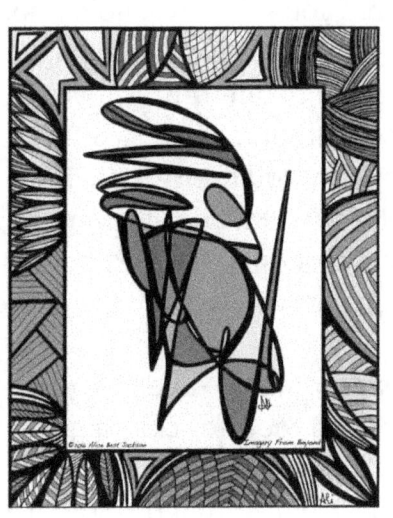

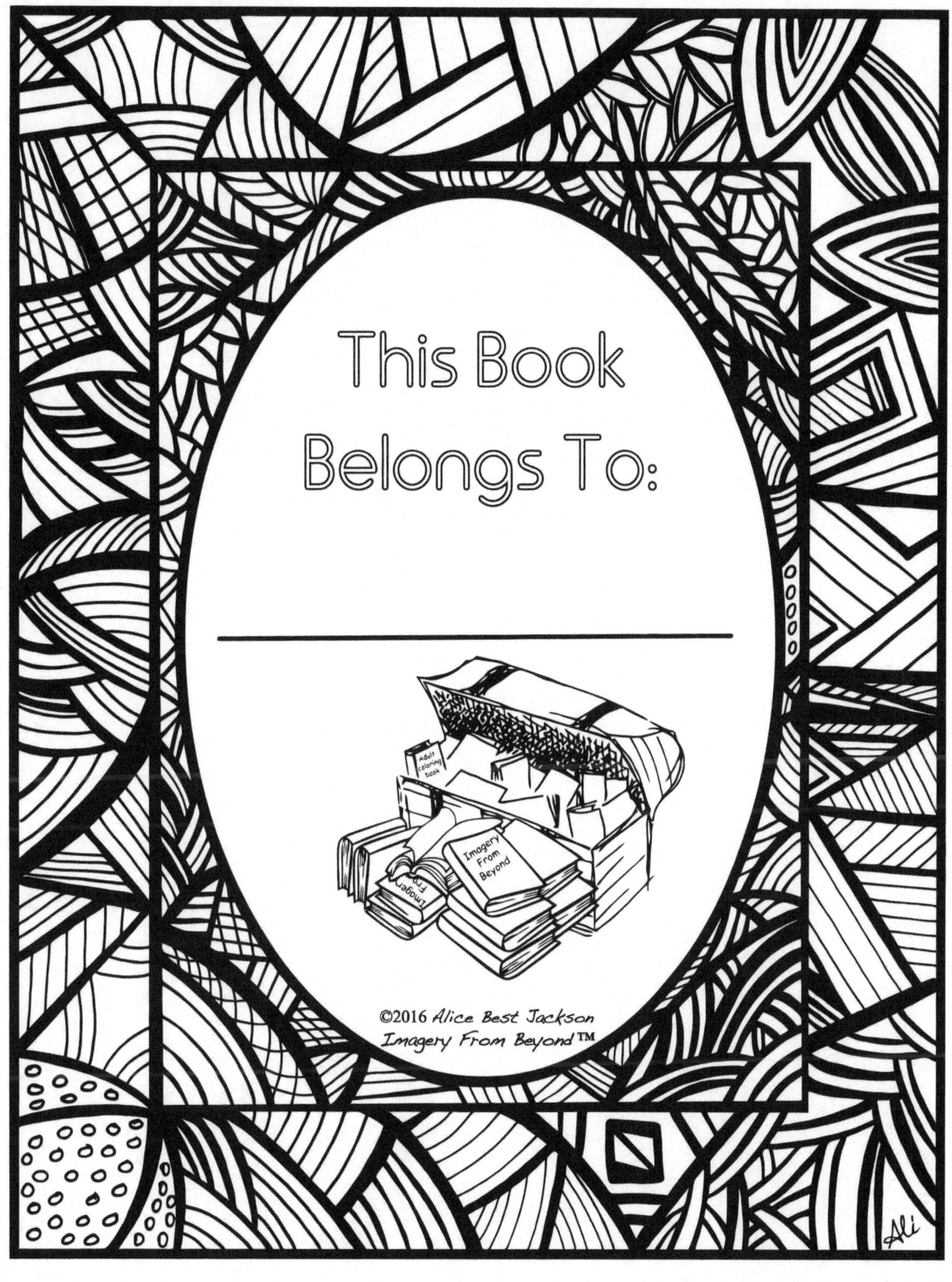

This Book

Belongs To:

_____

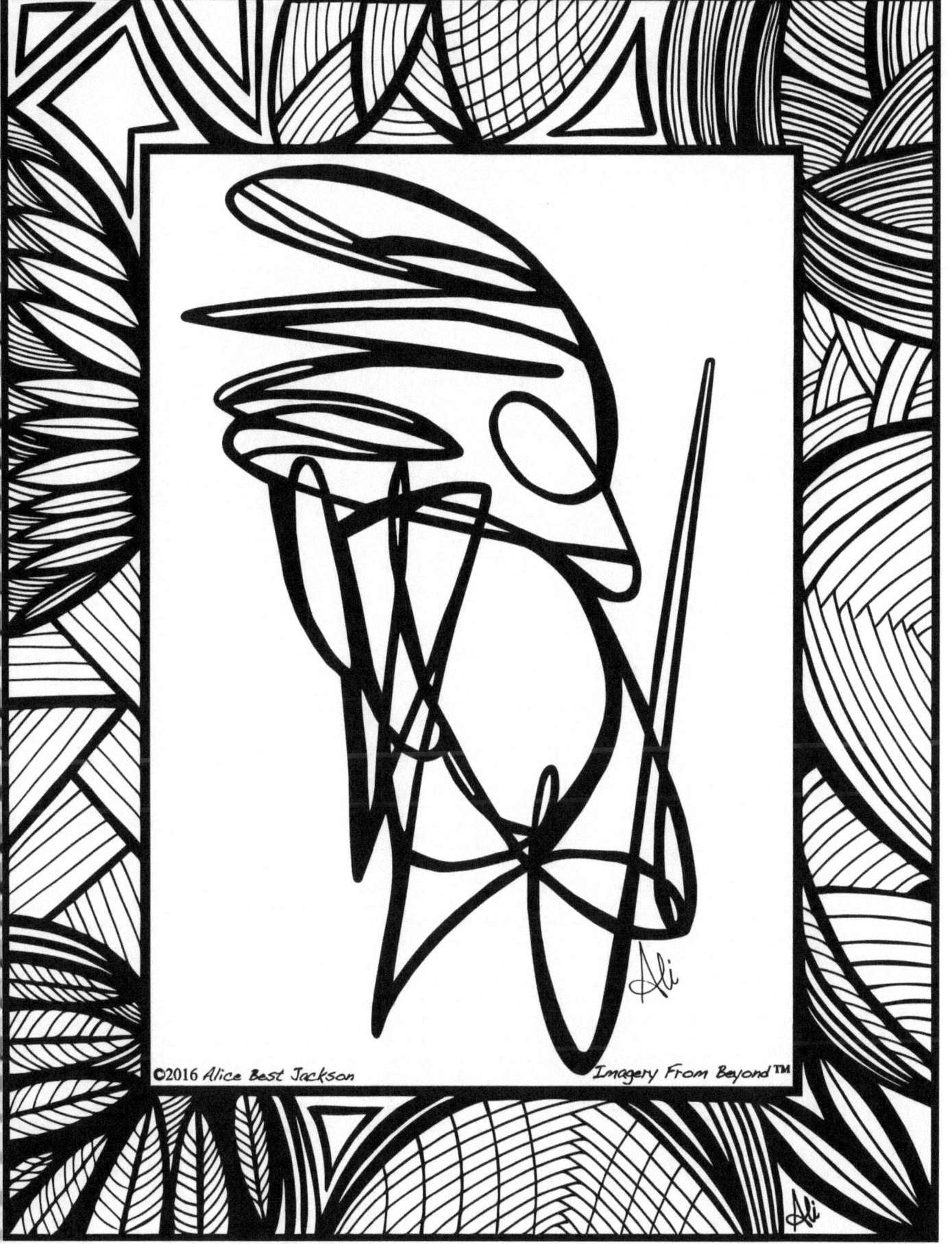

©2016 Alice Best Jackson

Imagery From Beyond™

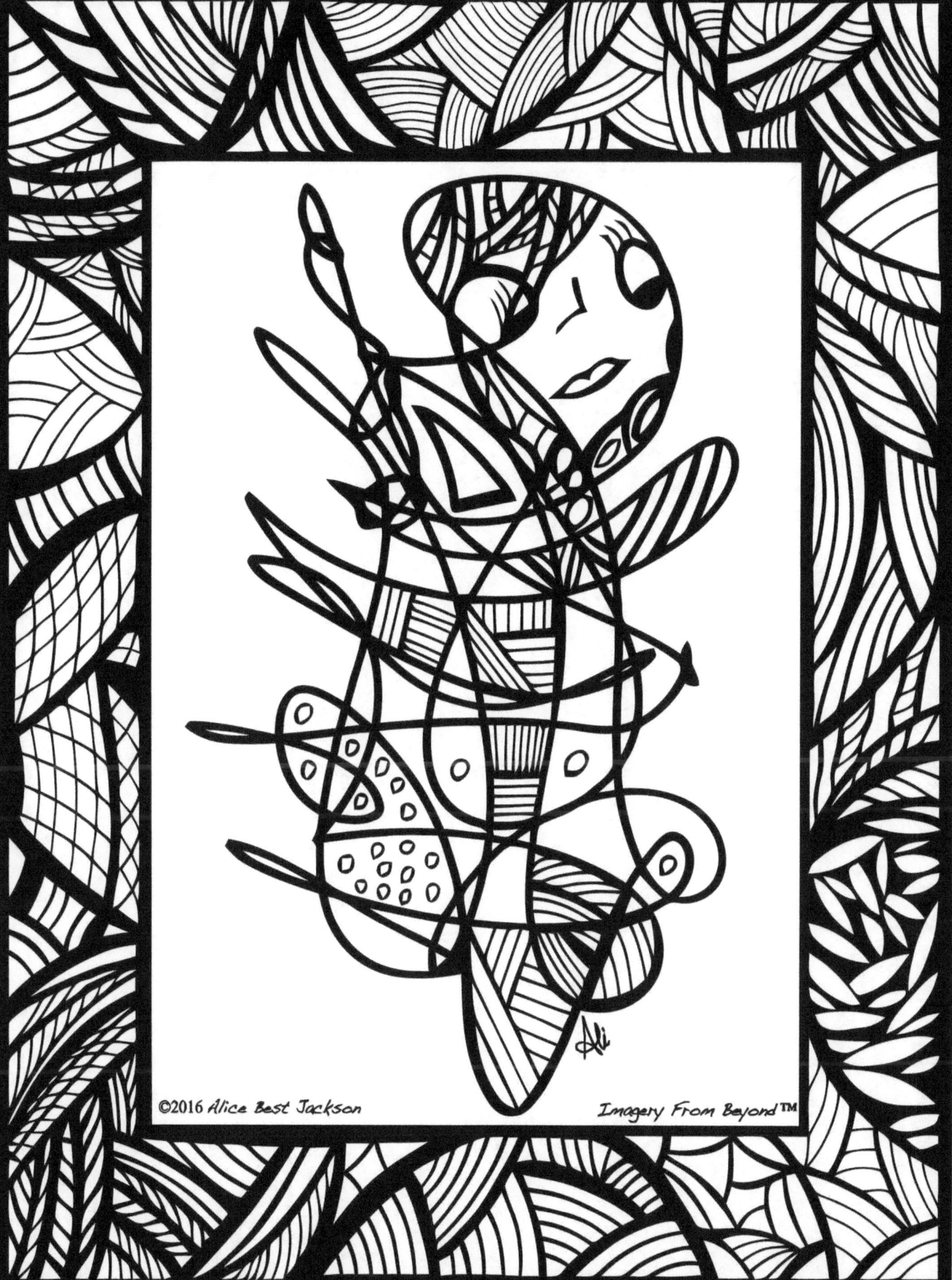

©2016 Alice Best Jackson

Imagery From Beyond™

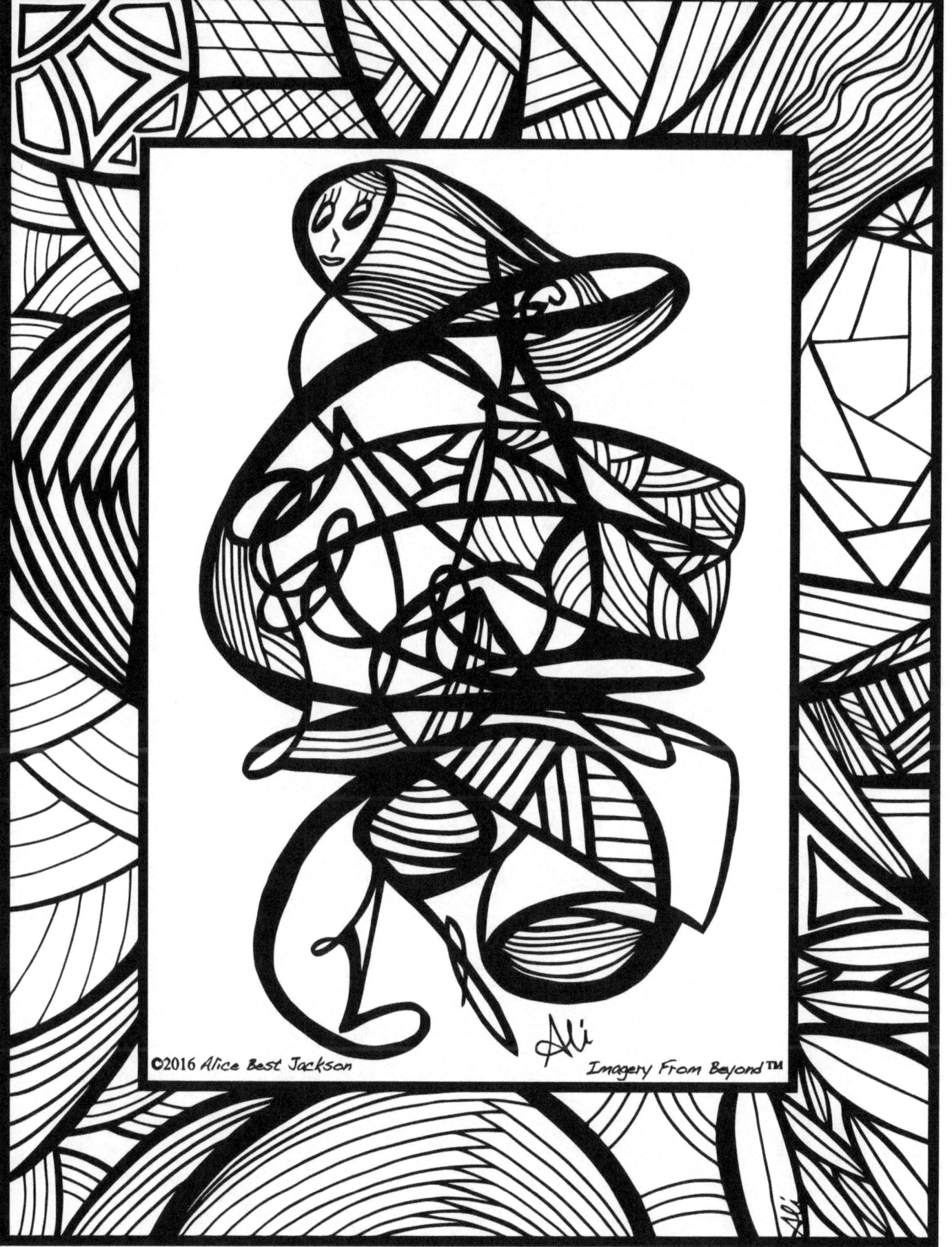

©2016 Alice Best Jackson

Imagery From Beyond™

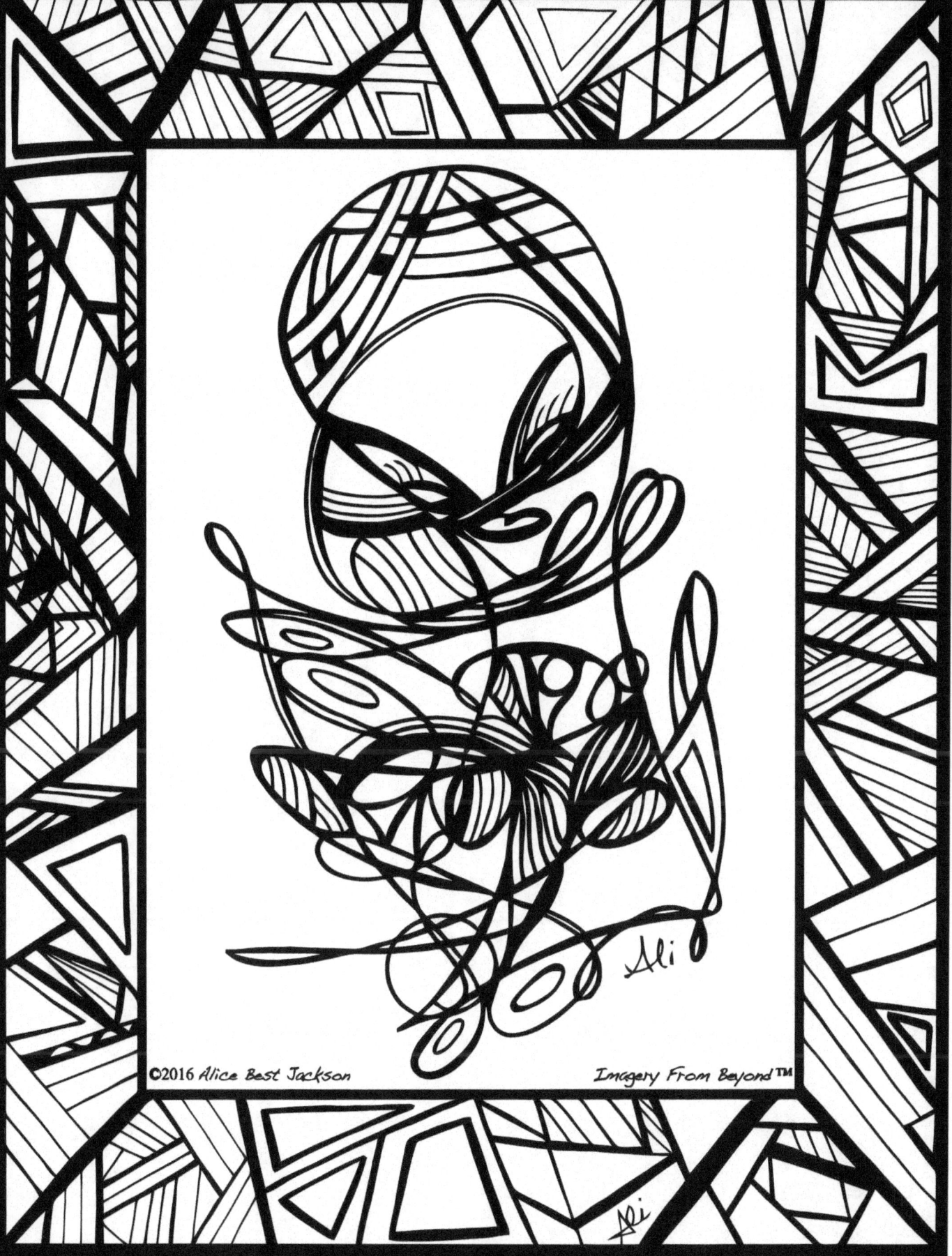

©2016 Alice Best Jackson

Imagery From Beyond™

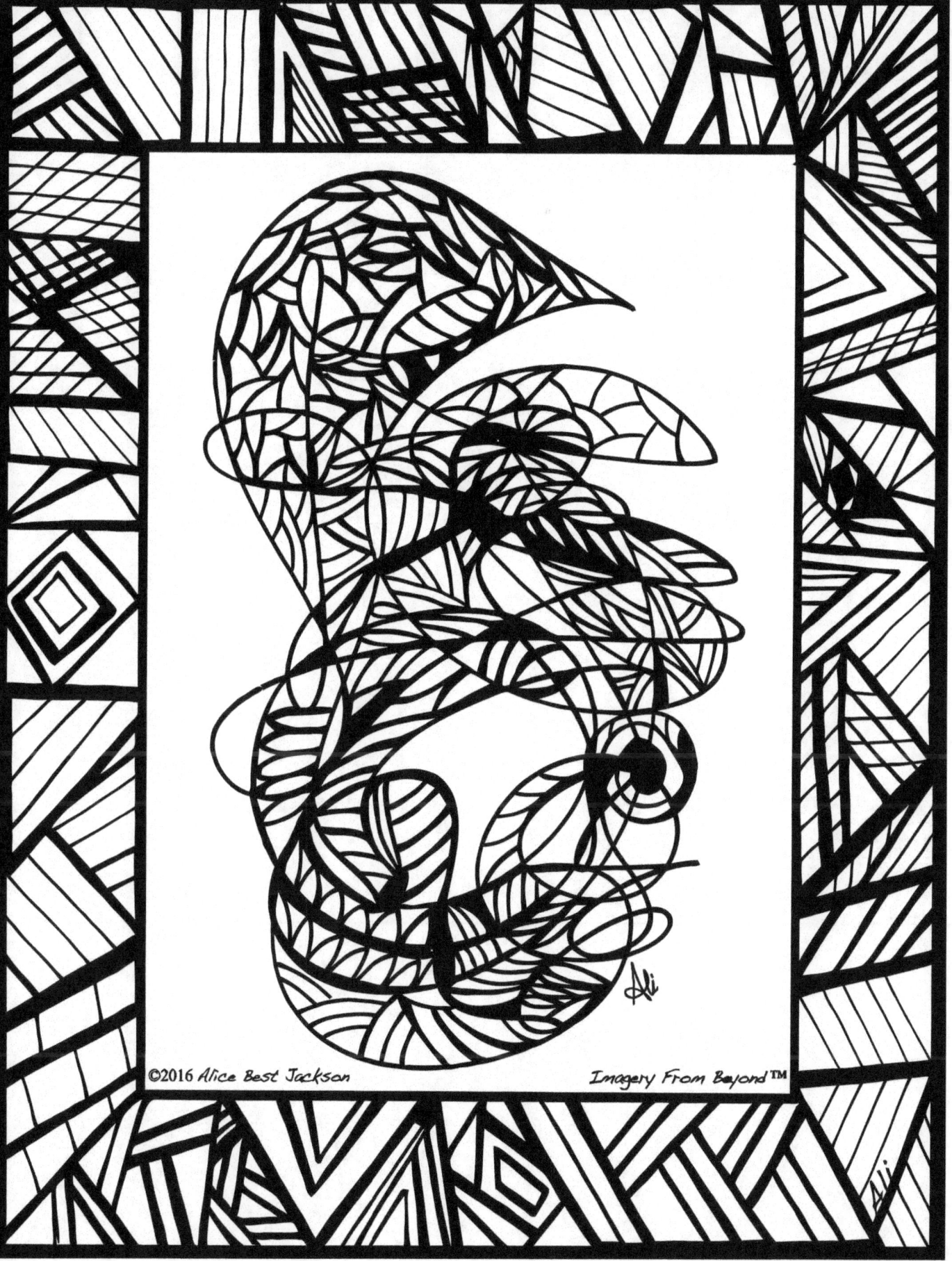

©2016 Alice Best Jackson

Imagery From Beyond™

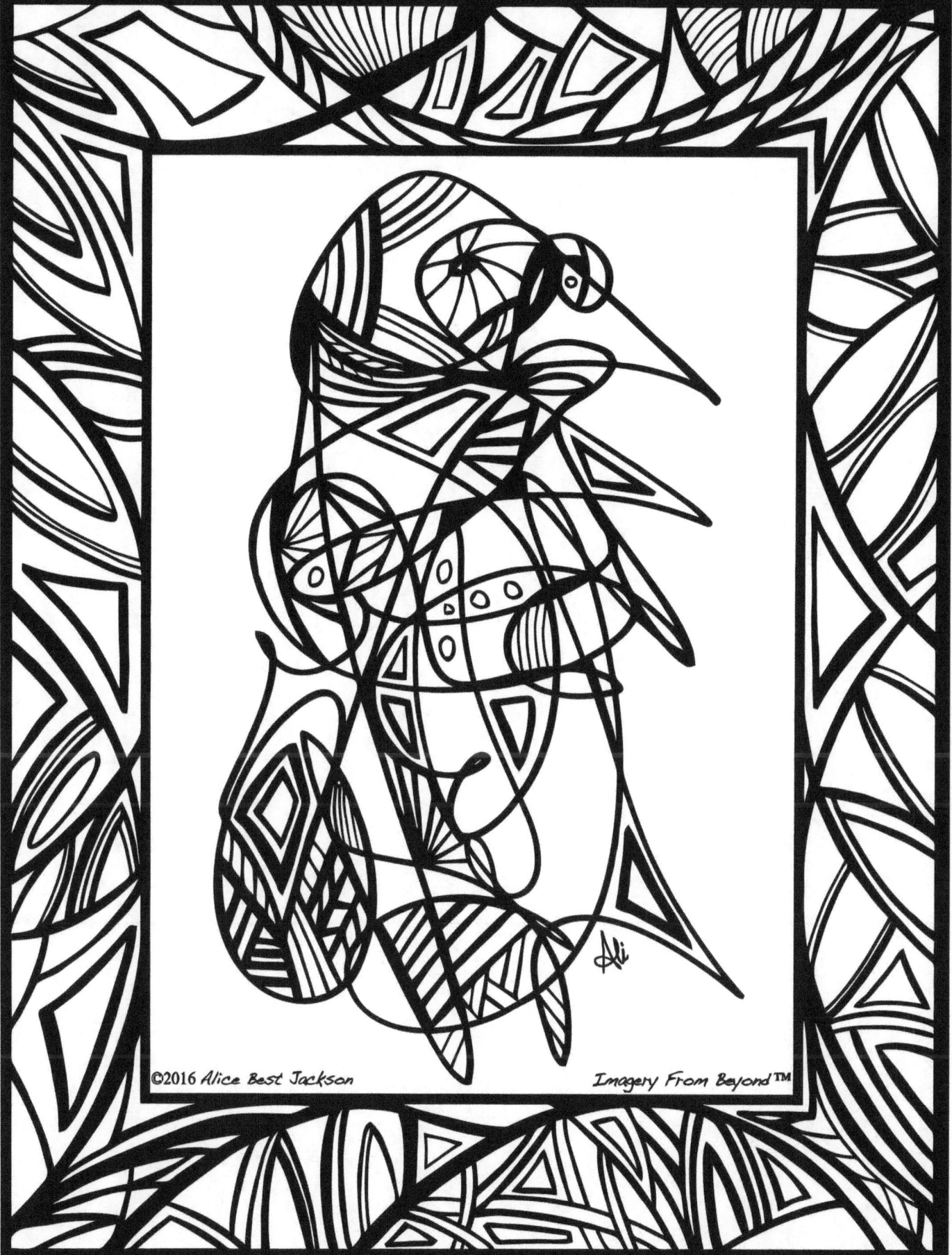

Imagery From Beyond™

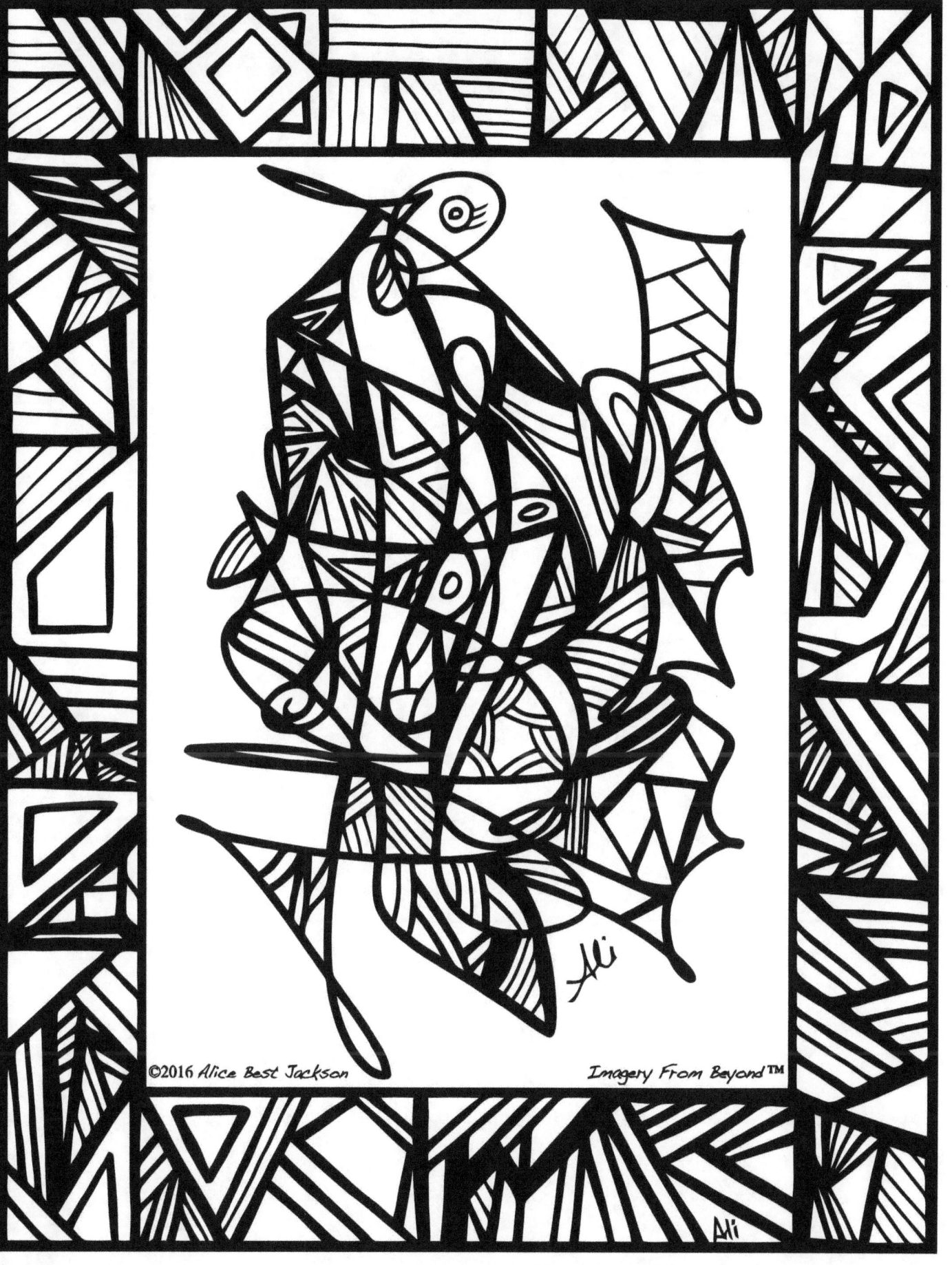

©2016 Alice Best Jackson

Imagery From Beyond™

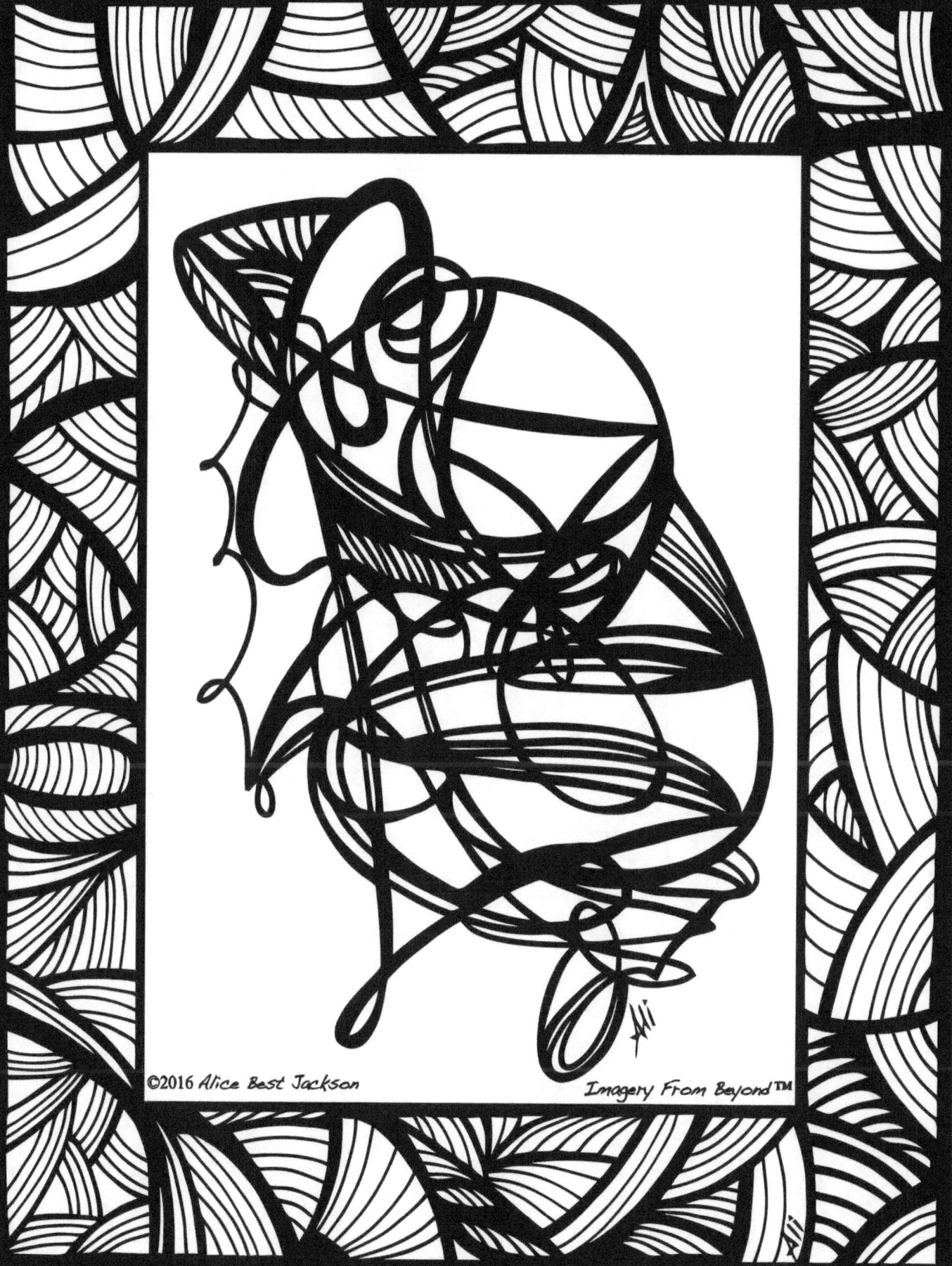

©2016 Alice Best Jackson

Imagery From Beyond™

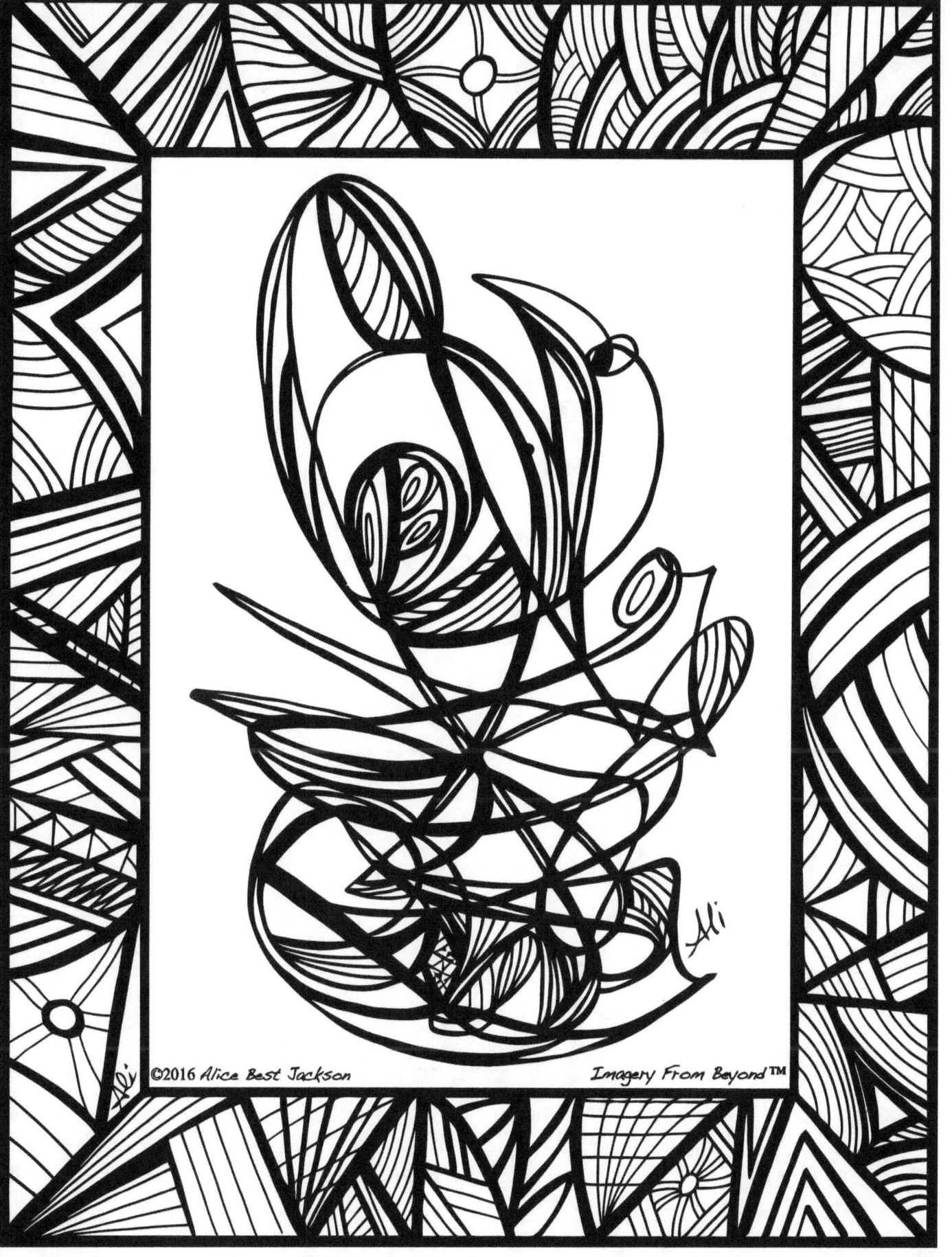

©2016 Alice Best Jackson

Imagery From Beyond™

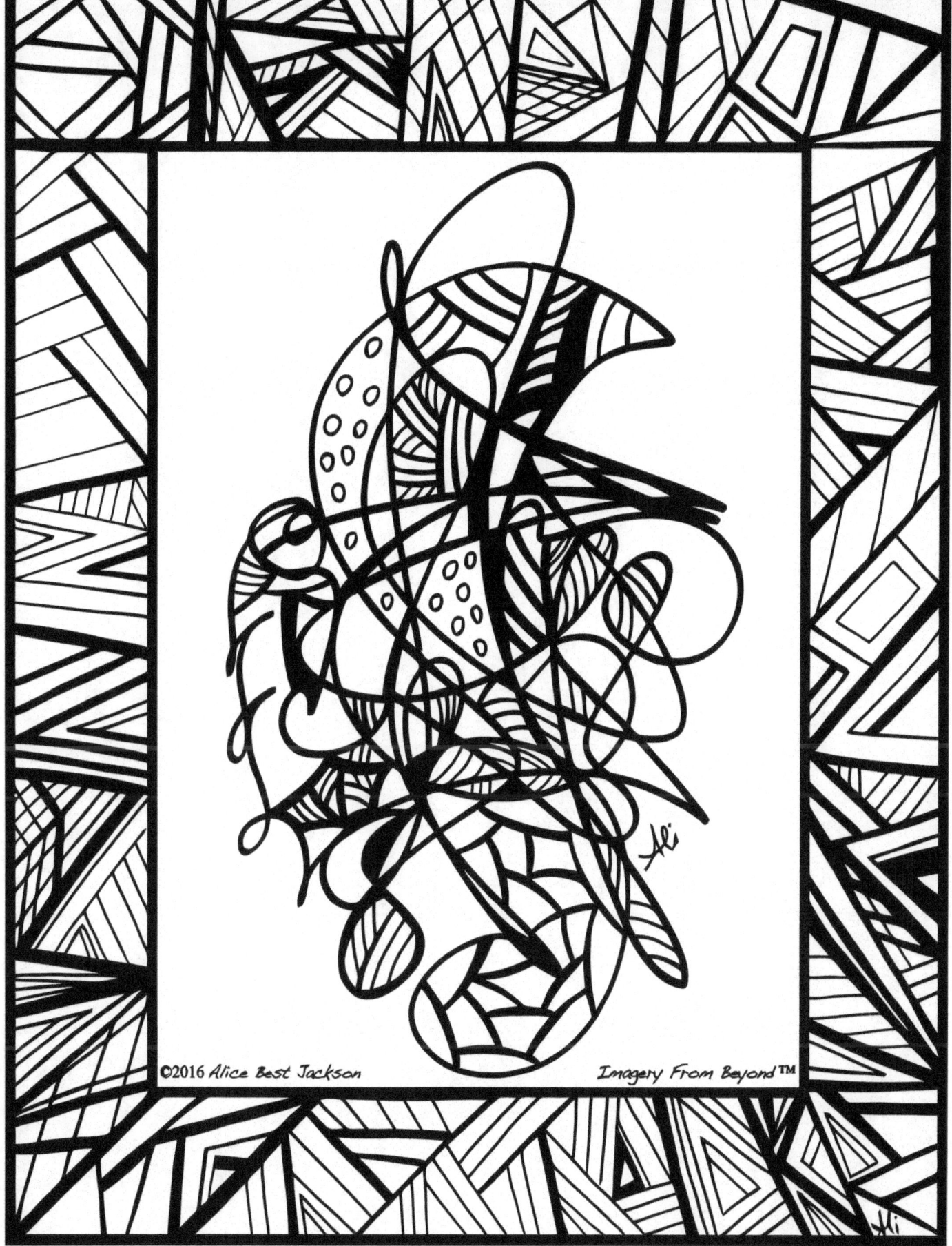

©2016 Alice Best Jackson

Imagery From Beyond™

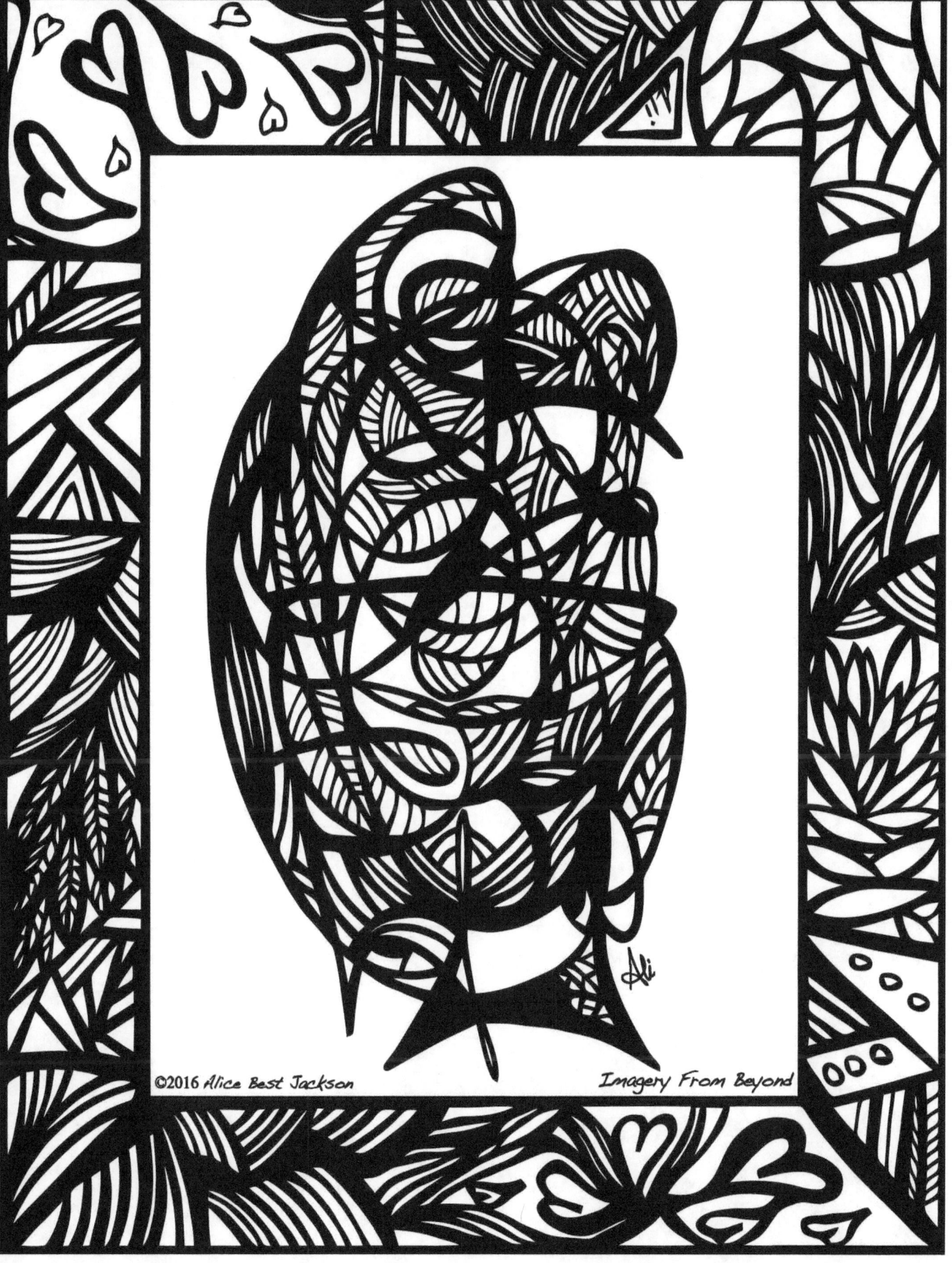

©2016 Alice Best Jackson

Imagery From Beyond

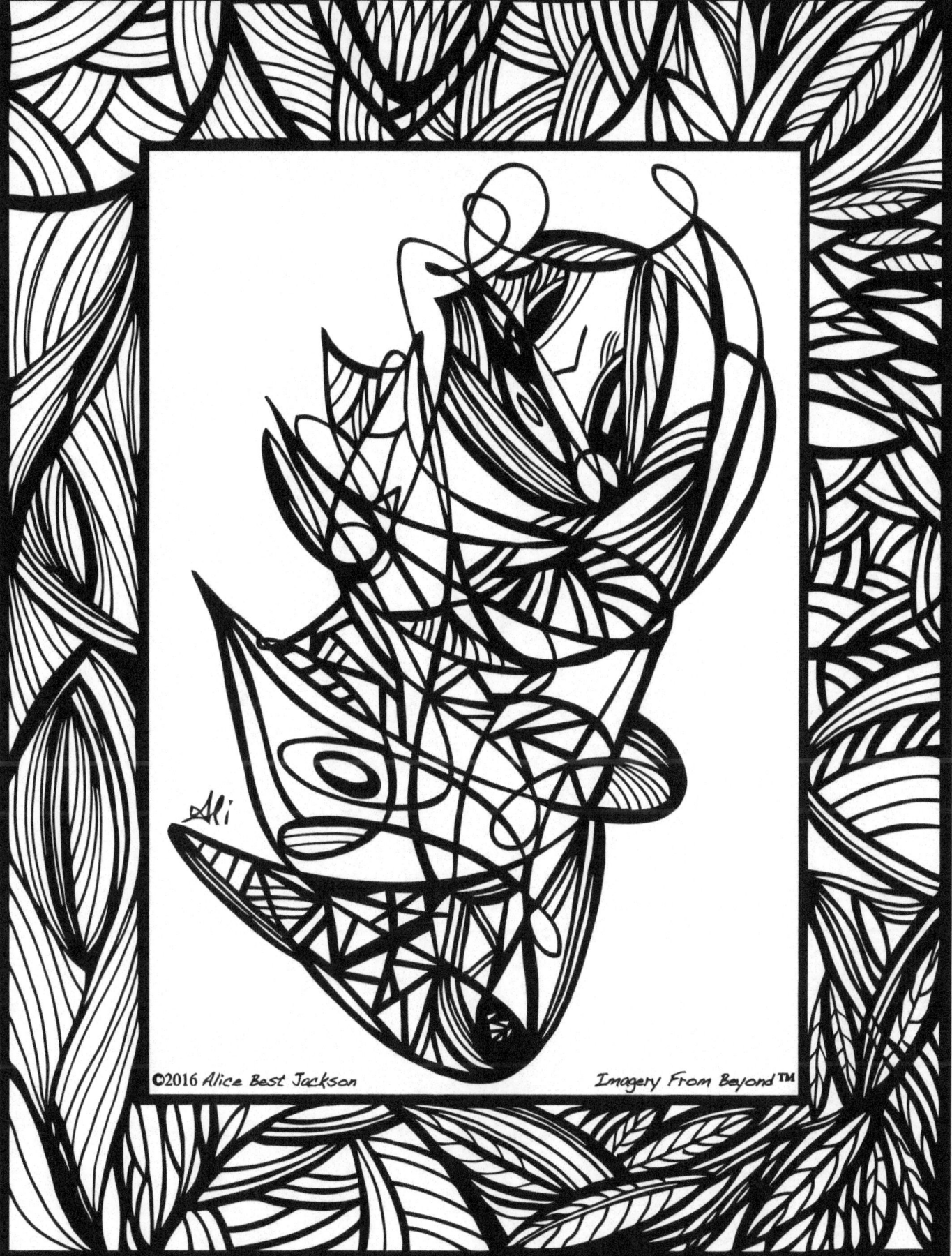

©2016 Alice Best Jackson

Imagery From Beyond™

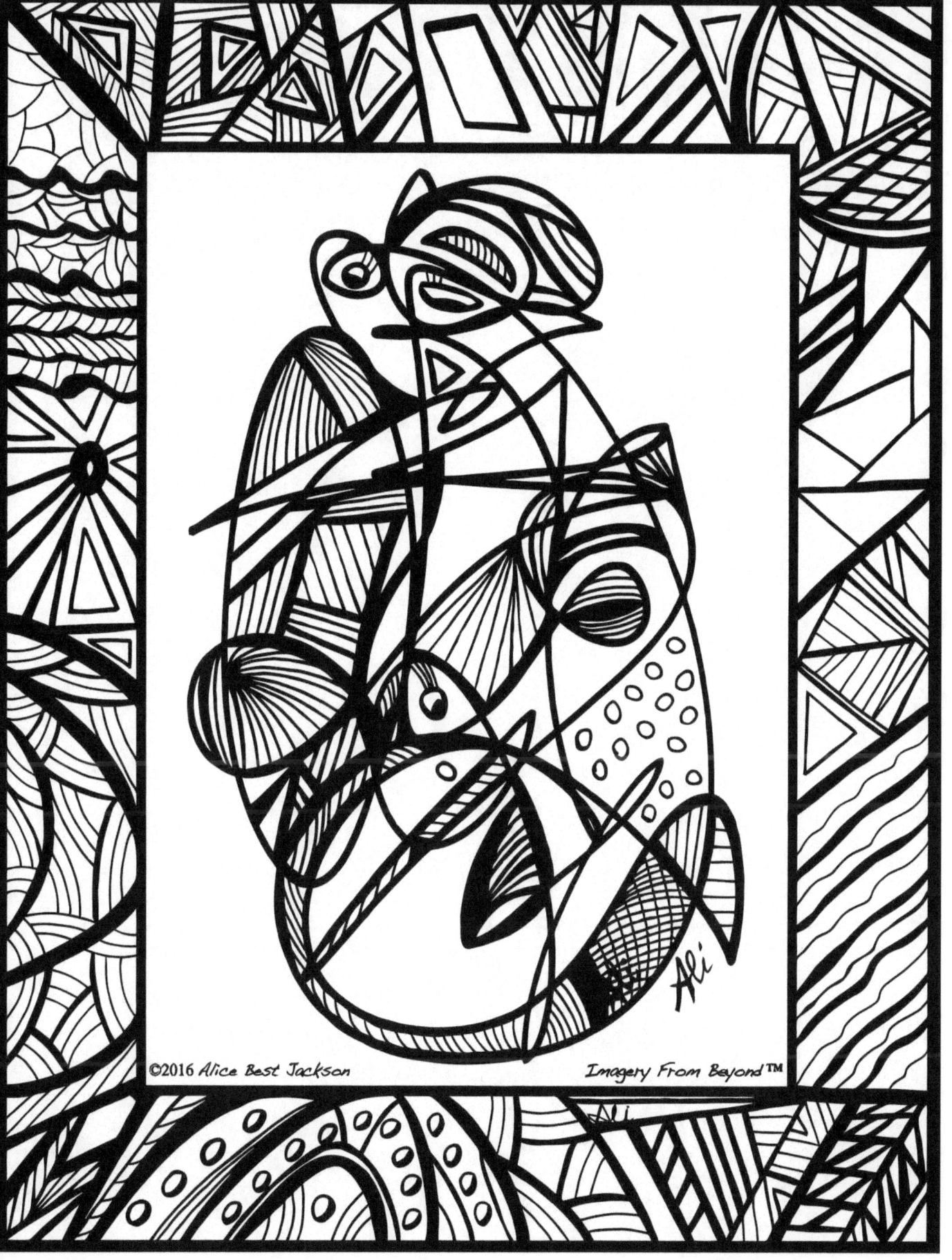

©2016 Alice Best Jackson

Imagery From Beyond™

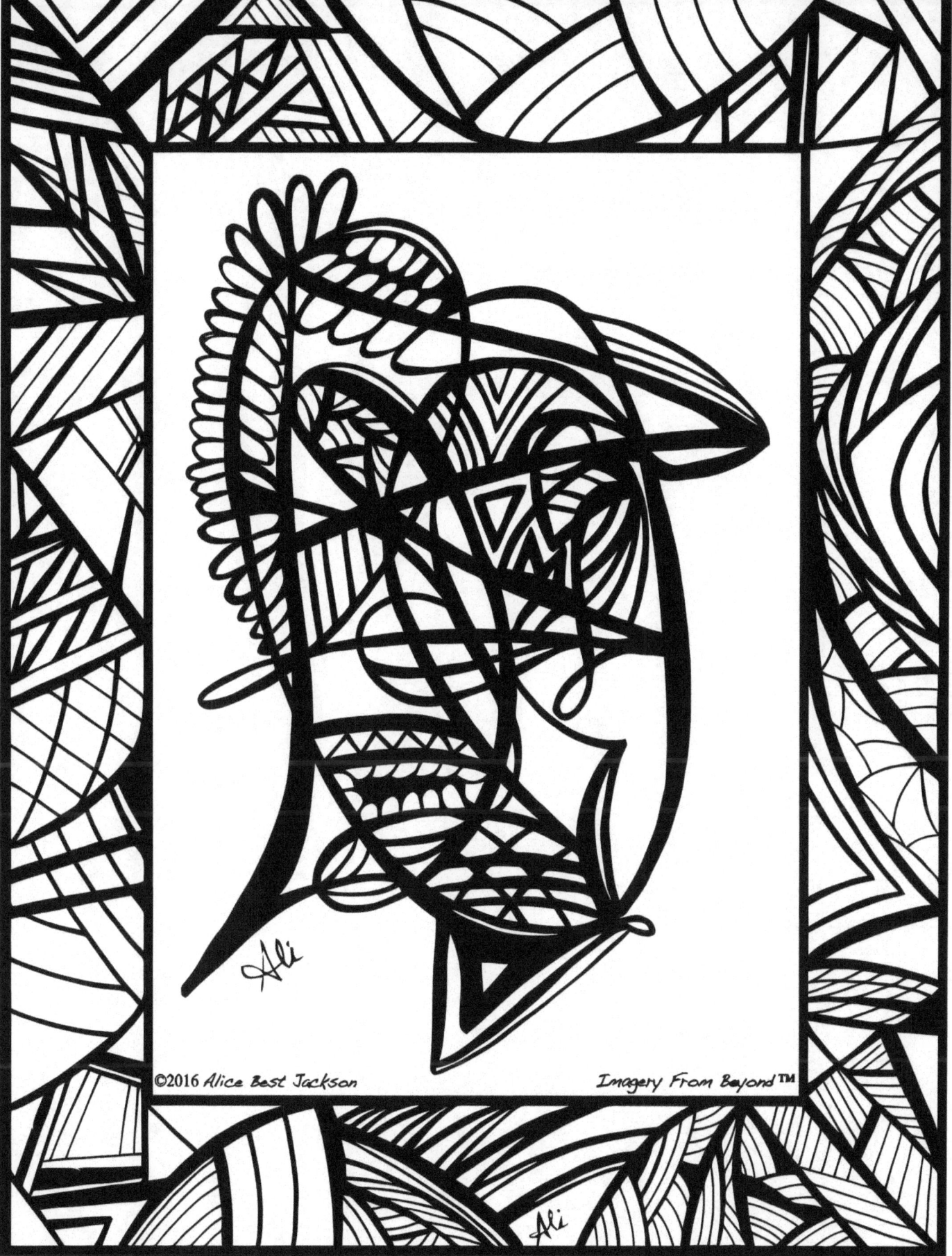

©2016 Alice Best Jackson

Imagery From Beyond™

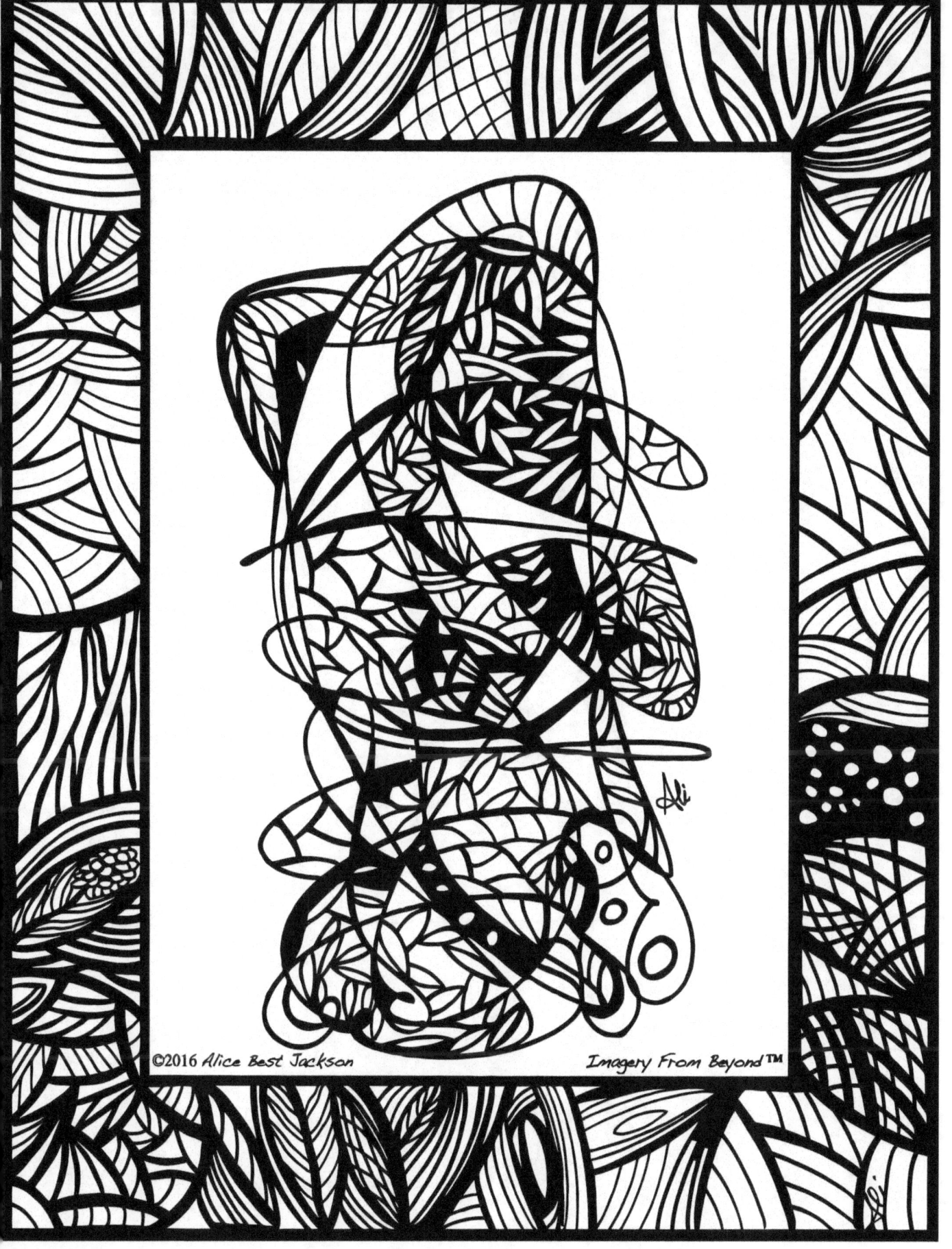

©2016 Alice Best Jackson

Imagery From Beyond™

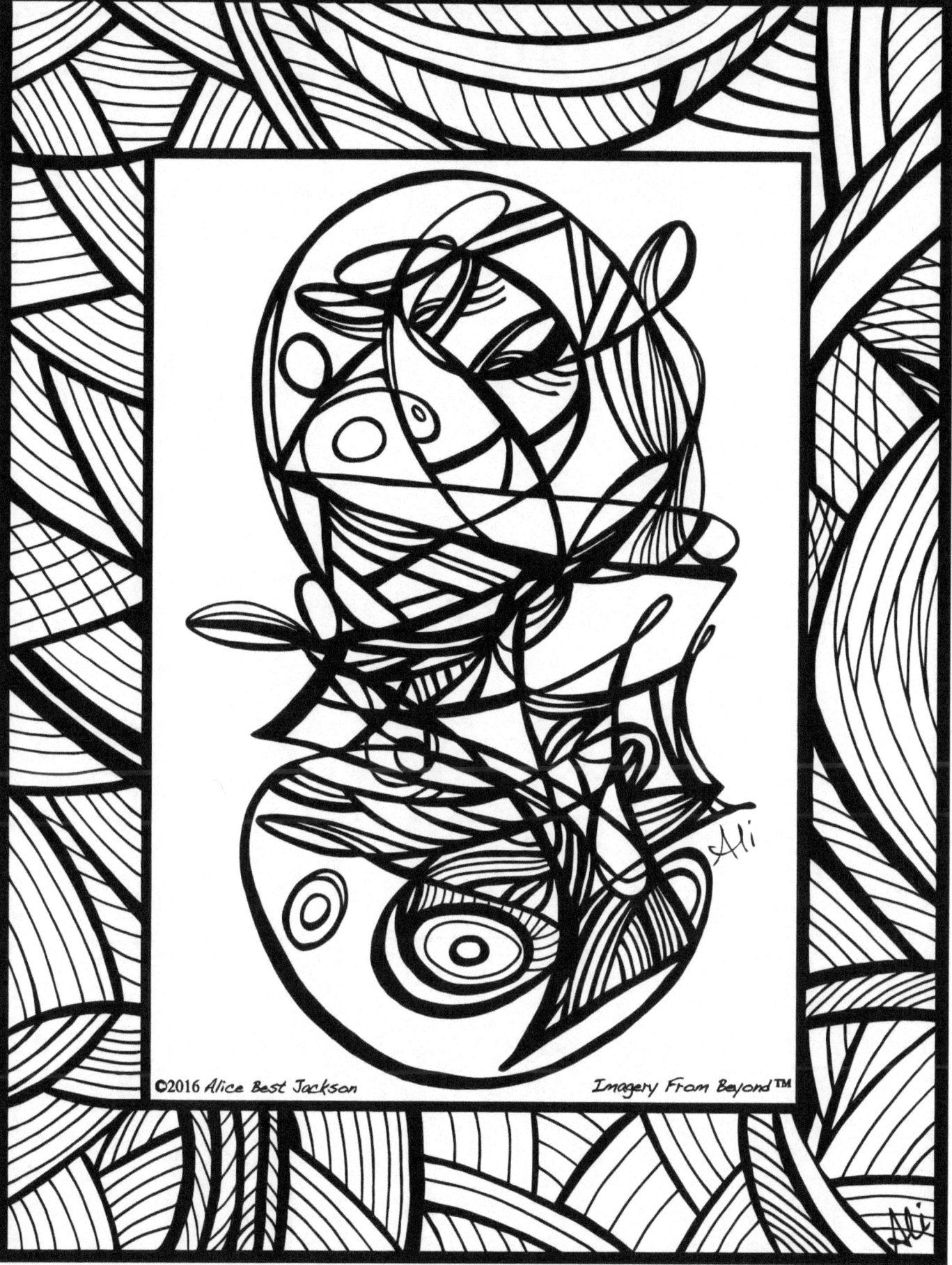

©2016 Alice Best Jackson

Imagery From Beyond™

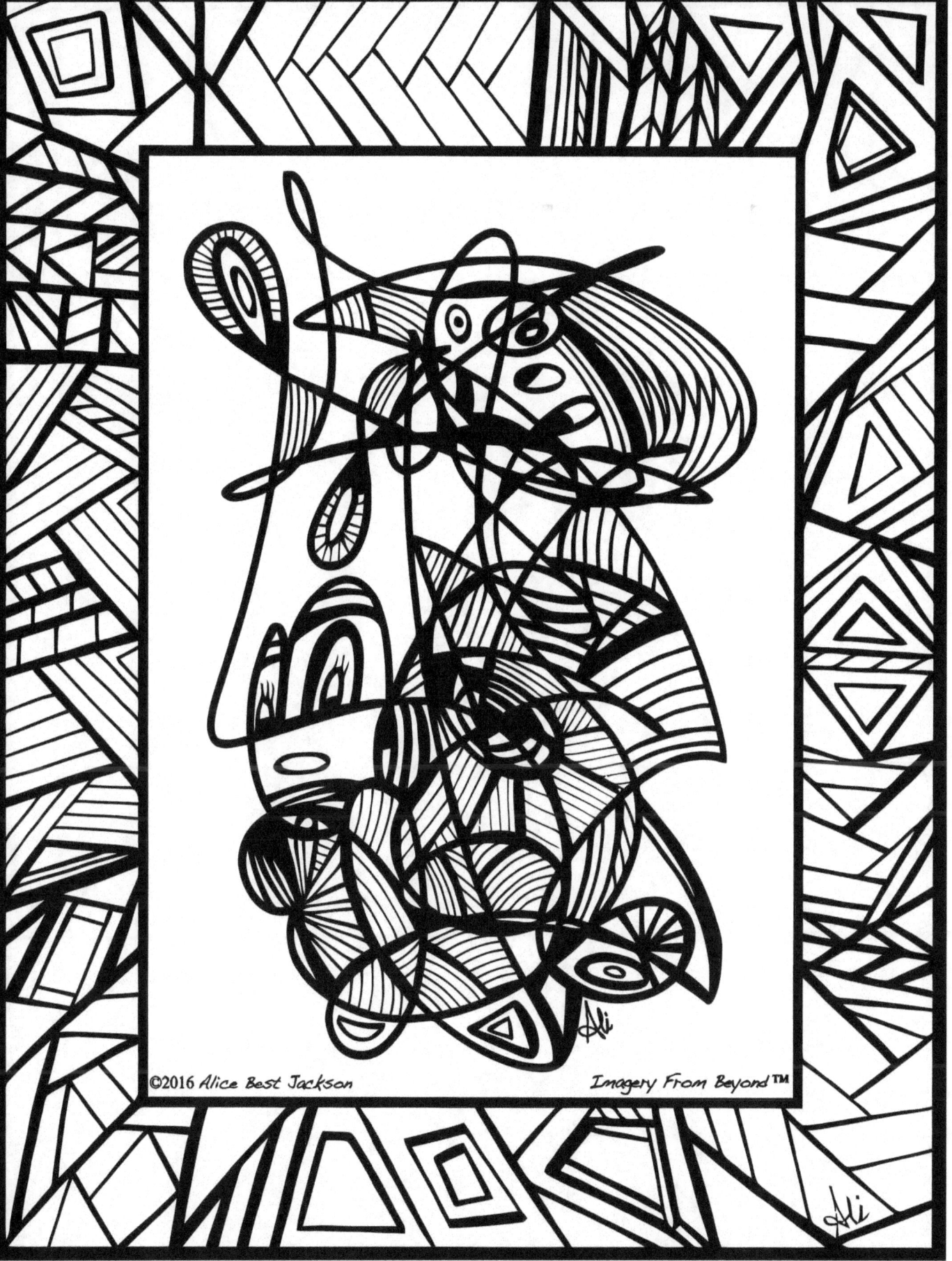

©2016 Alice Best Jackson

Imagery From Beyond™

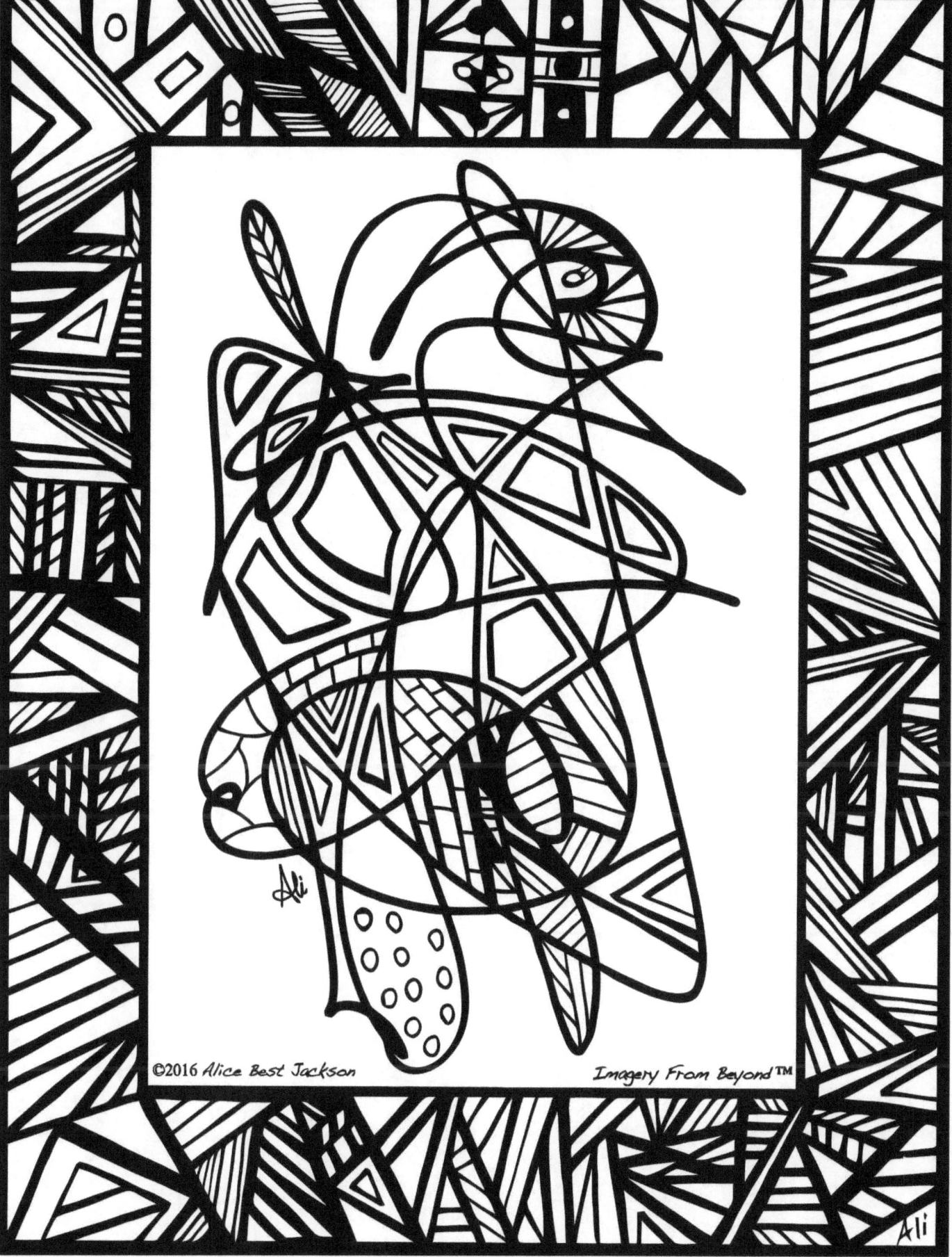

©2016 Alice Best Jackson

Imagery From Beyond™

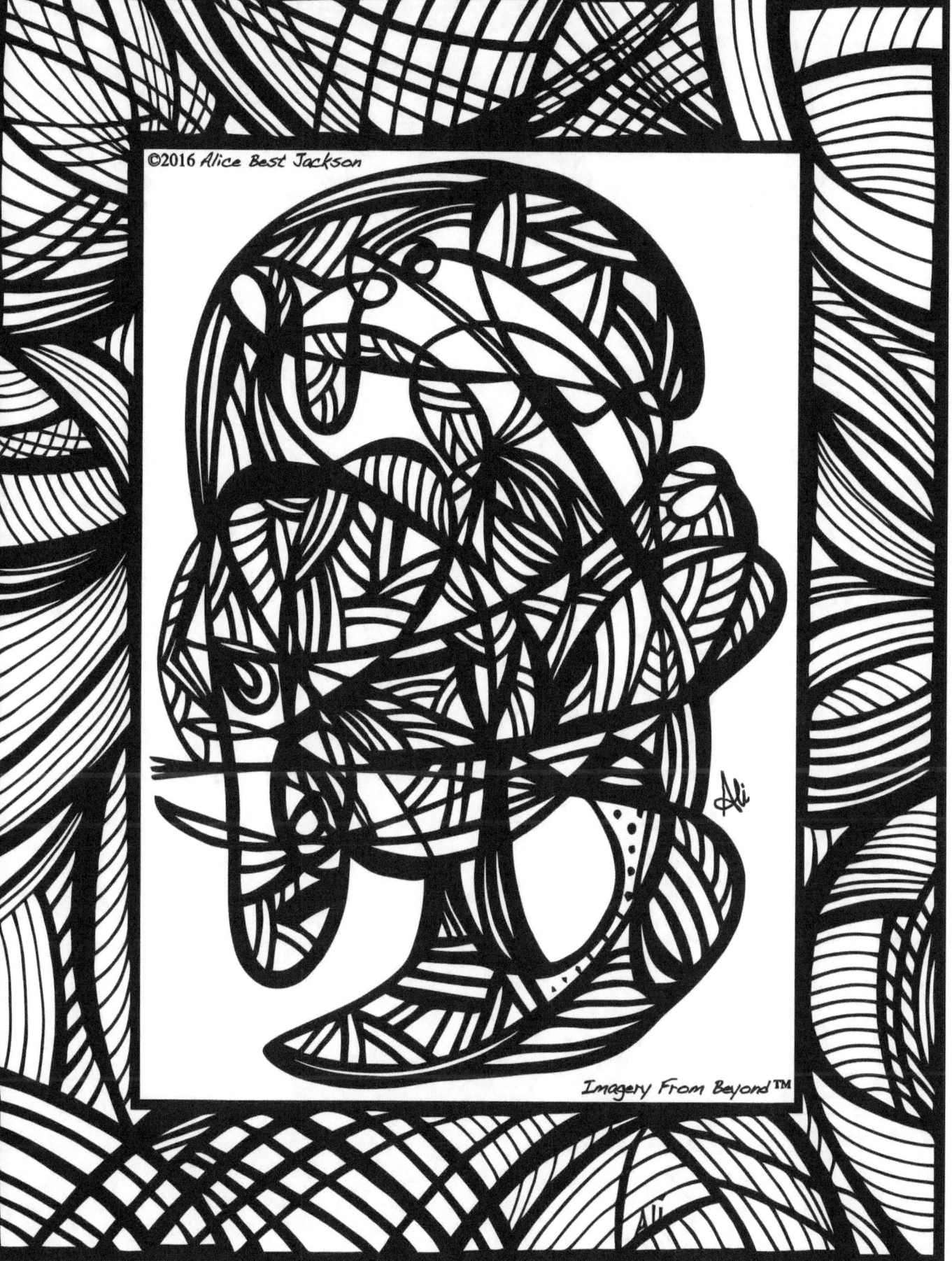

©2016 Alice Best Jackson

Imagery From Beyond™

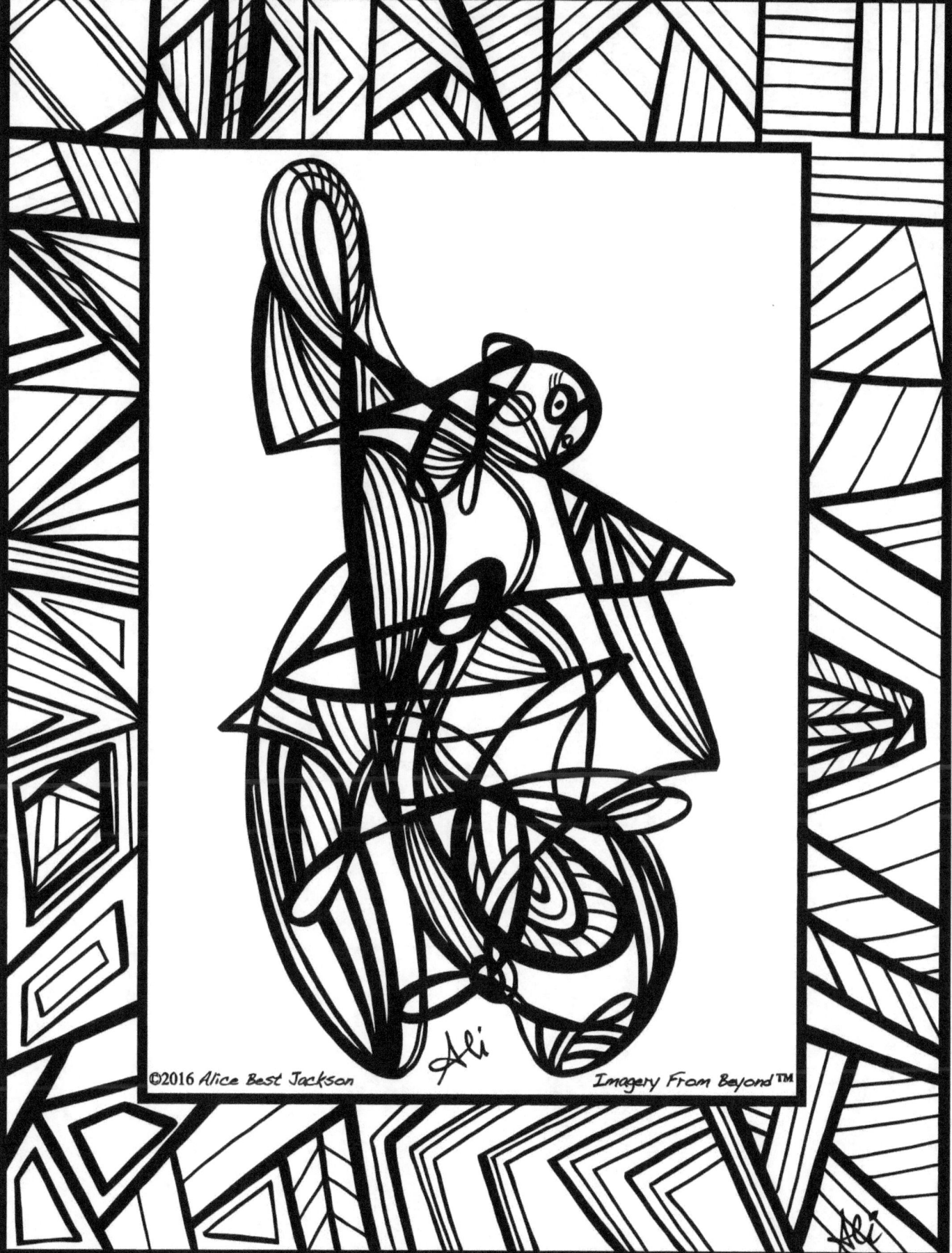

©2016 Alice Best Jackson

Imagery From Beyond™

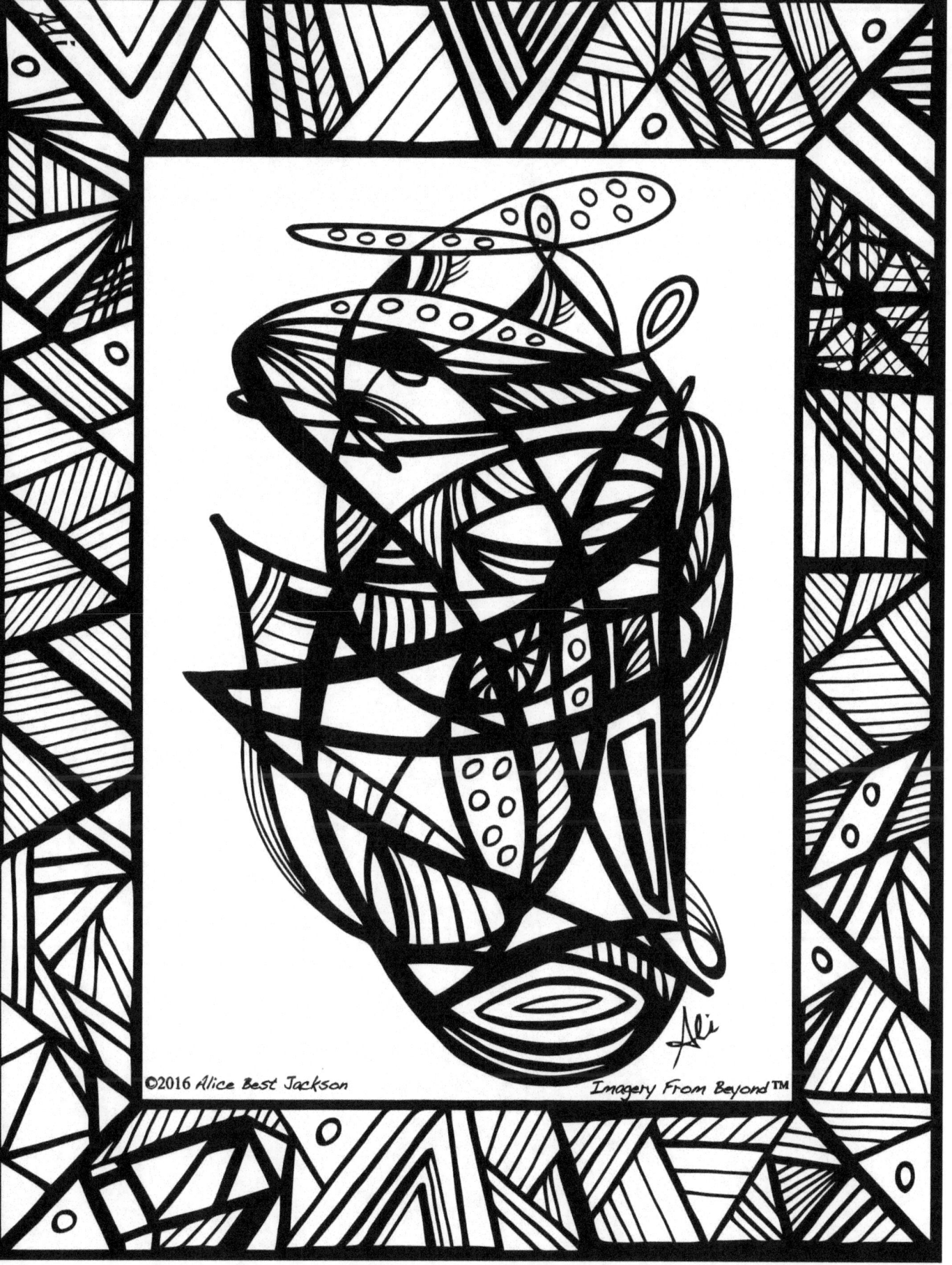

©2016 Alice Best Jackson

Imagery From Beyond™

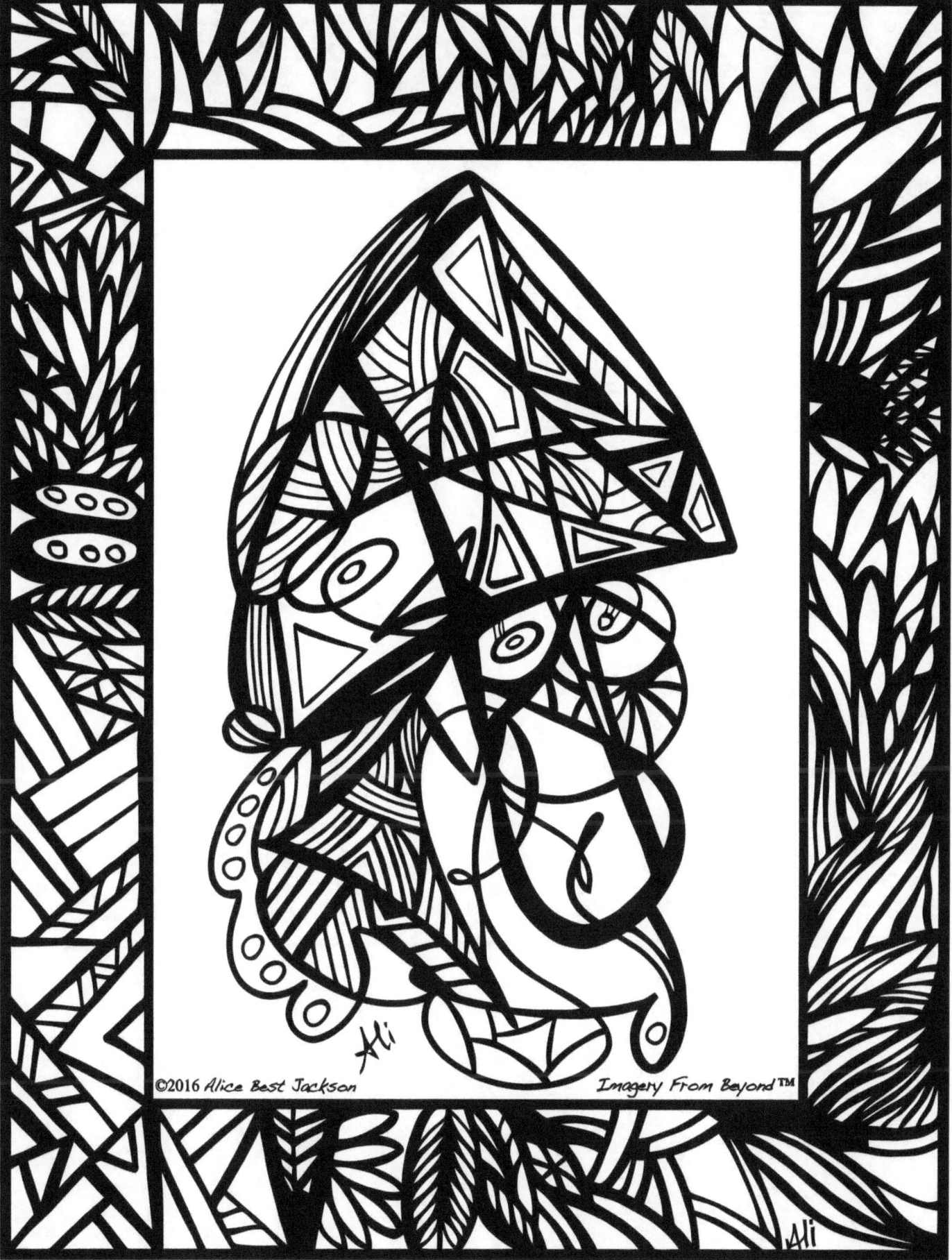

©2016 Alice Best Jackson   Imagery From Beyond™

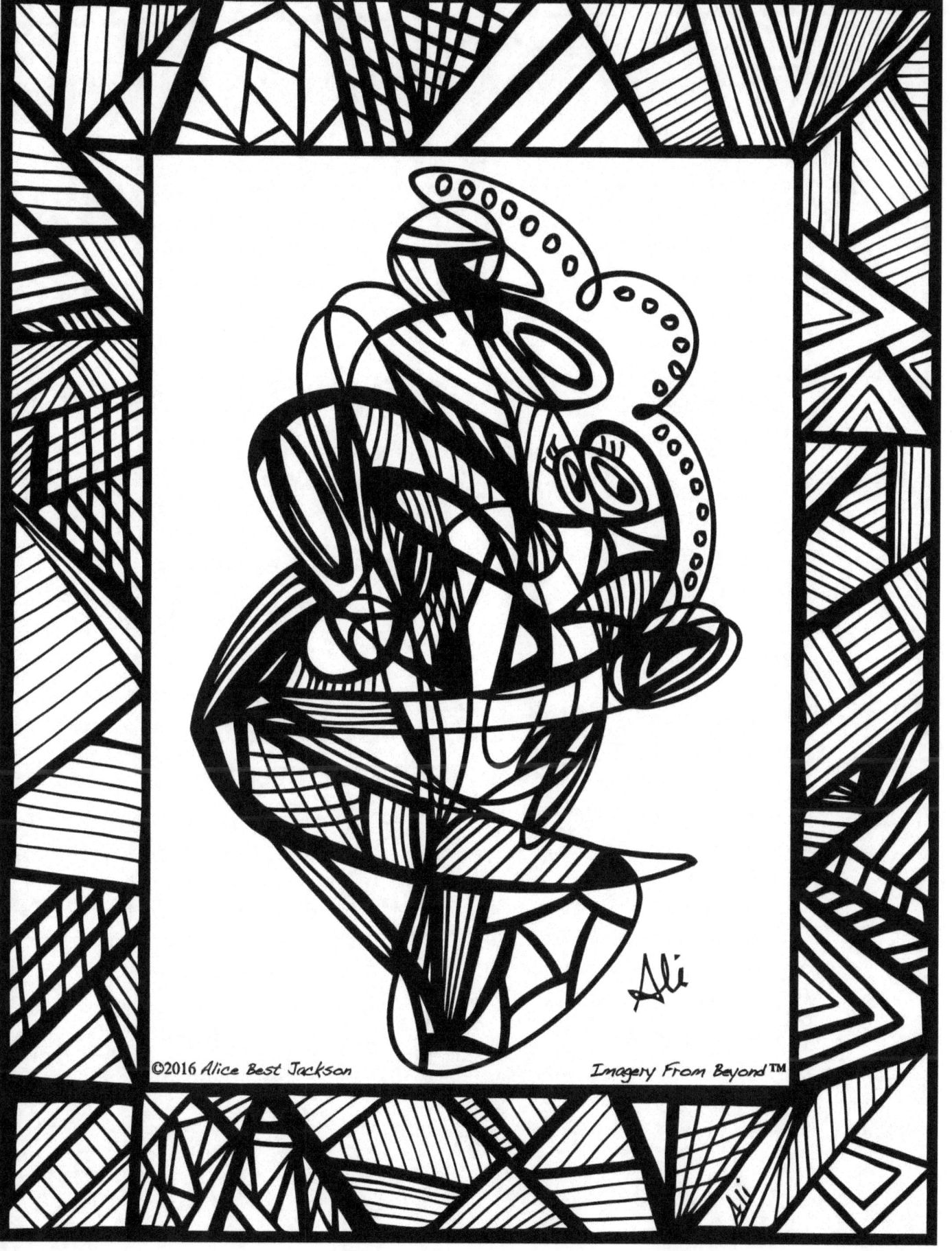

©2016 Alice Best Jackson

Imagery From Beyond™

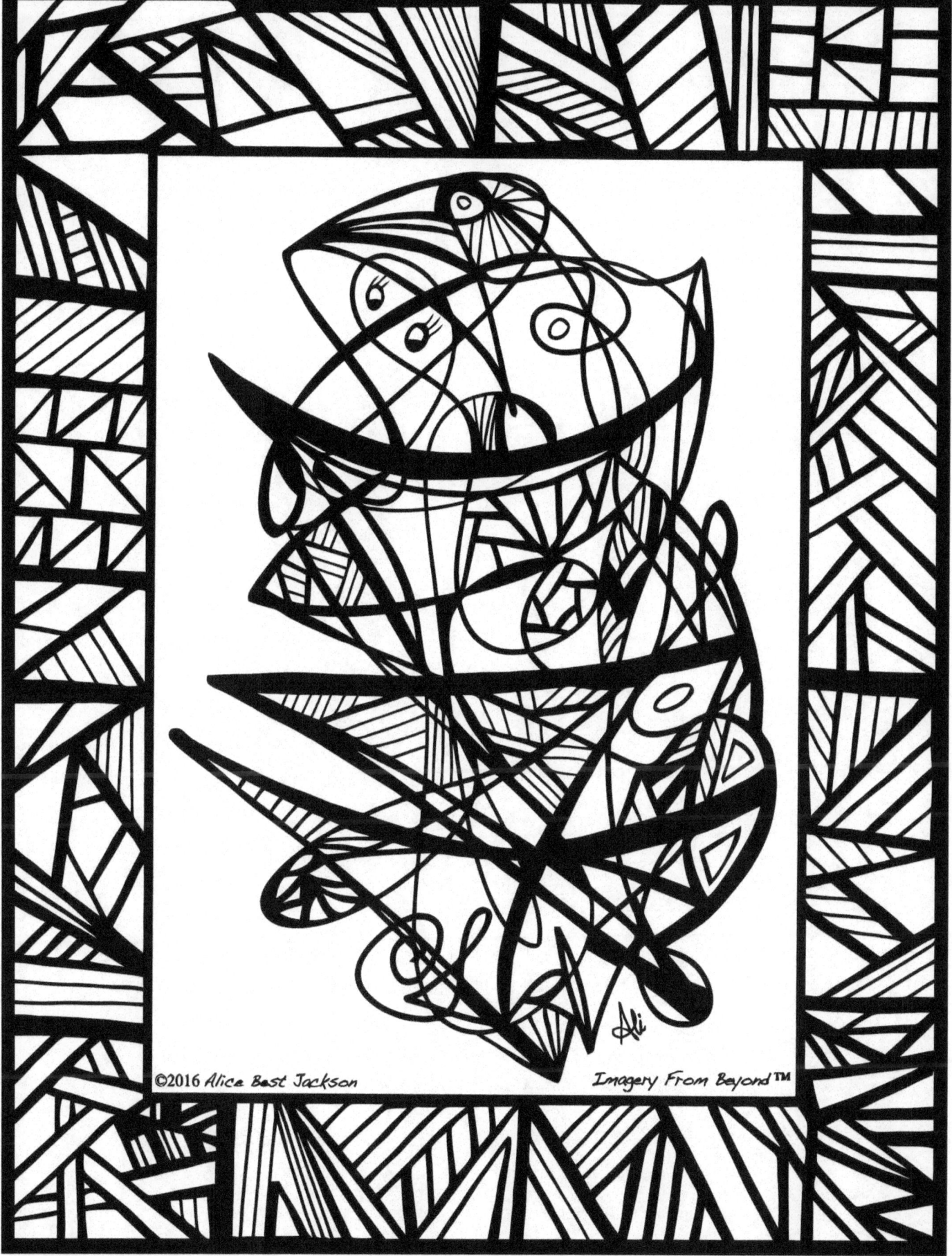

©2016 Alice Best Jackson

Imagery From Beyond™

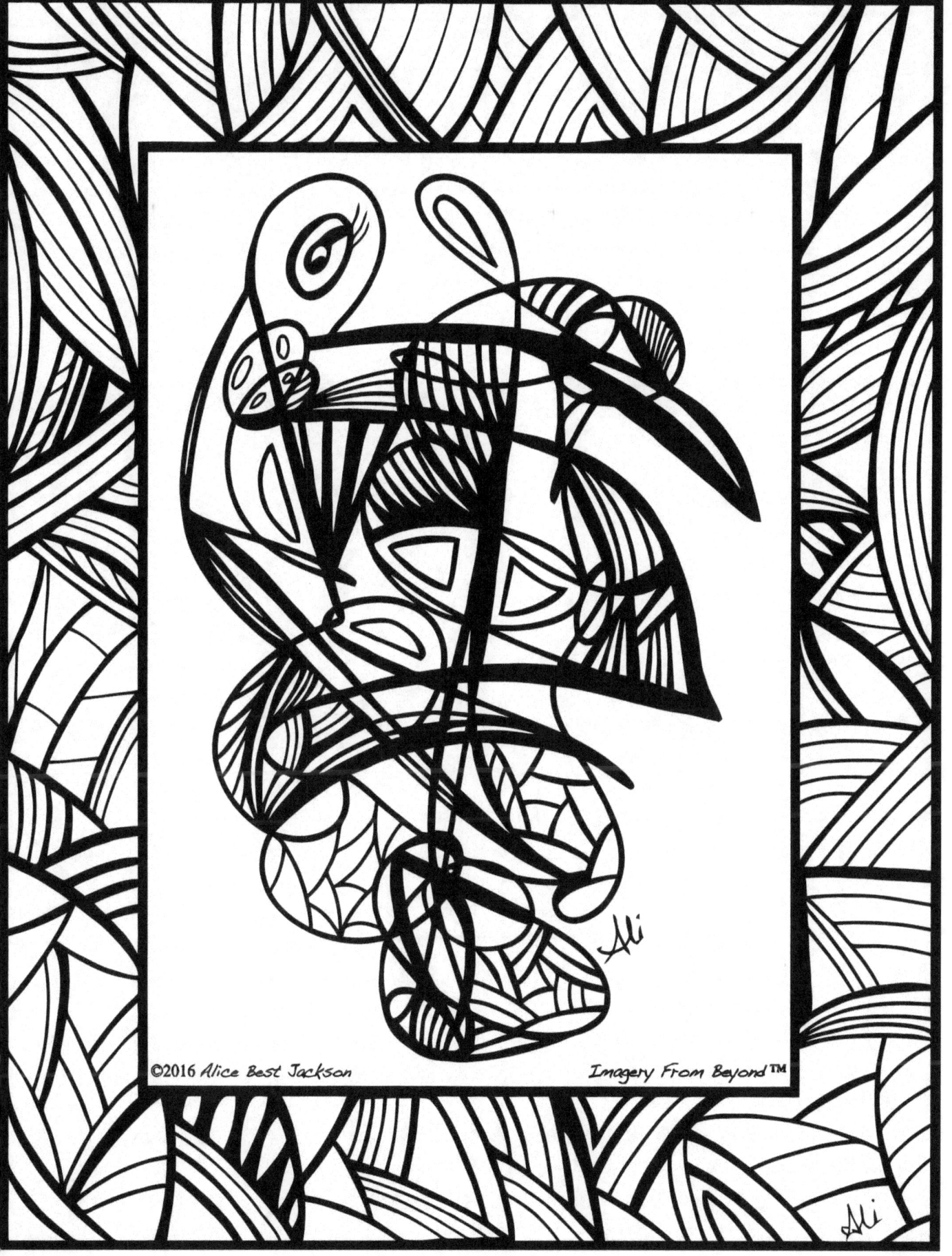

©2016 Alice Best Jackson

Imagery From Beyond™

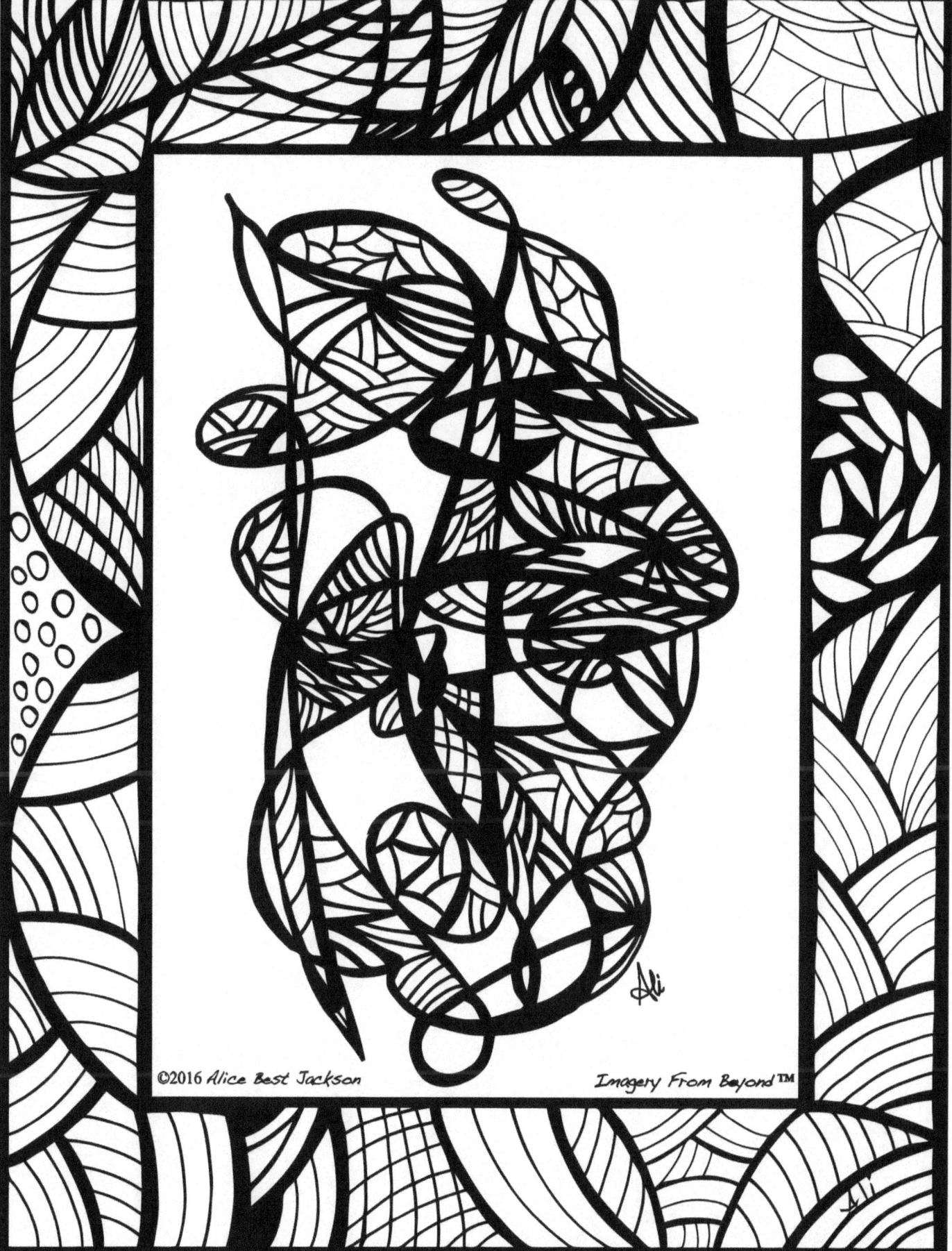

©2016 Alice Best Jackson

Imagery From Beyond™

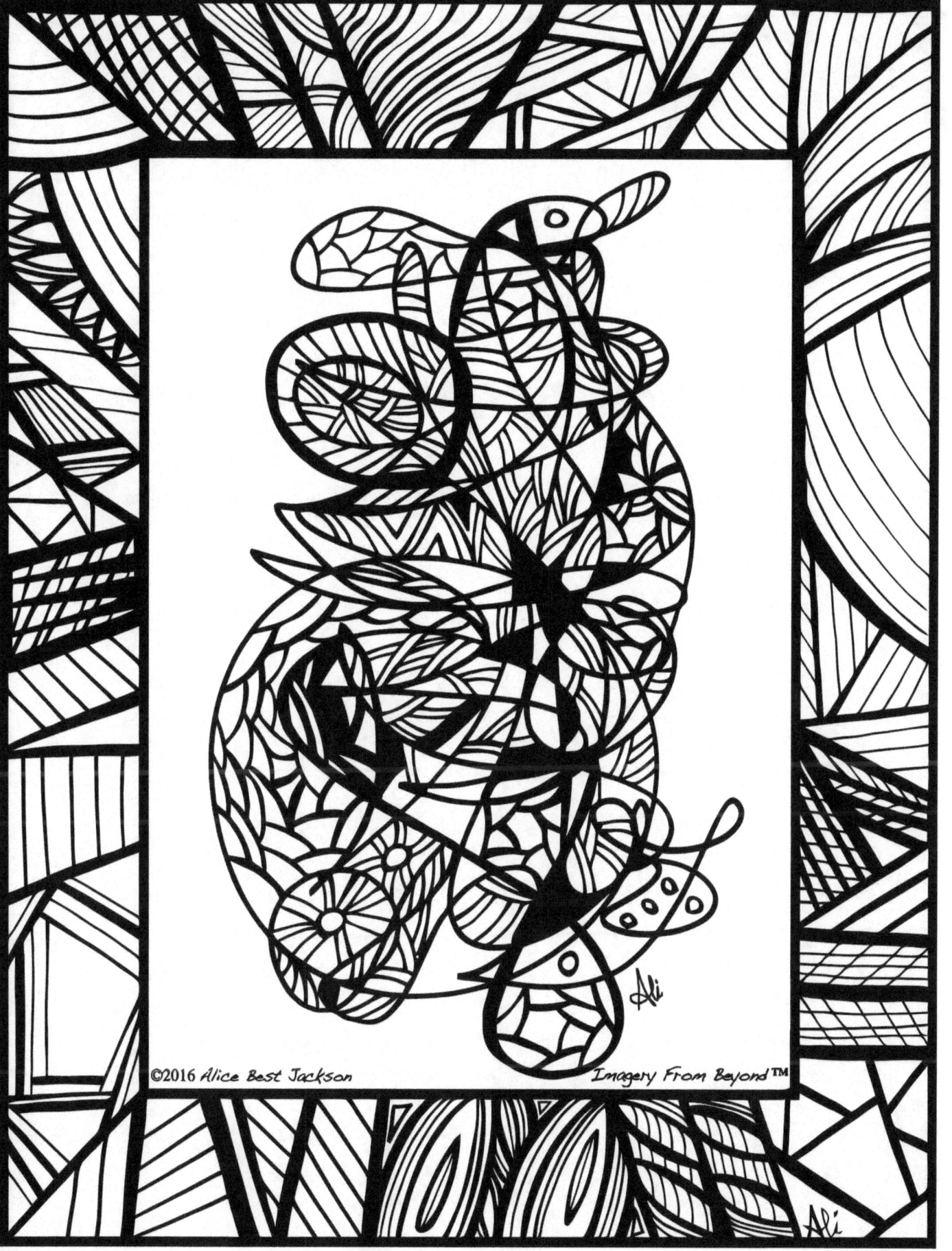

©2016 Alice Best Jackson

Imagery From Beyond™

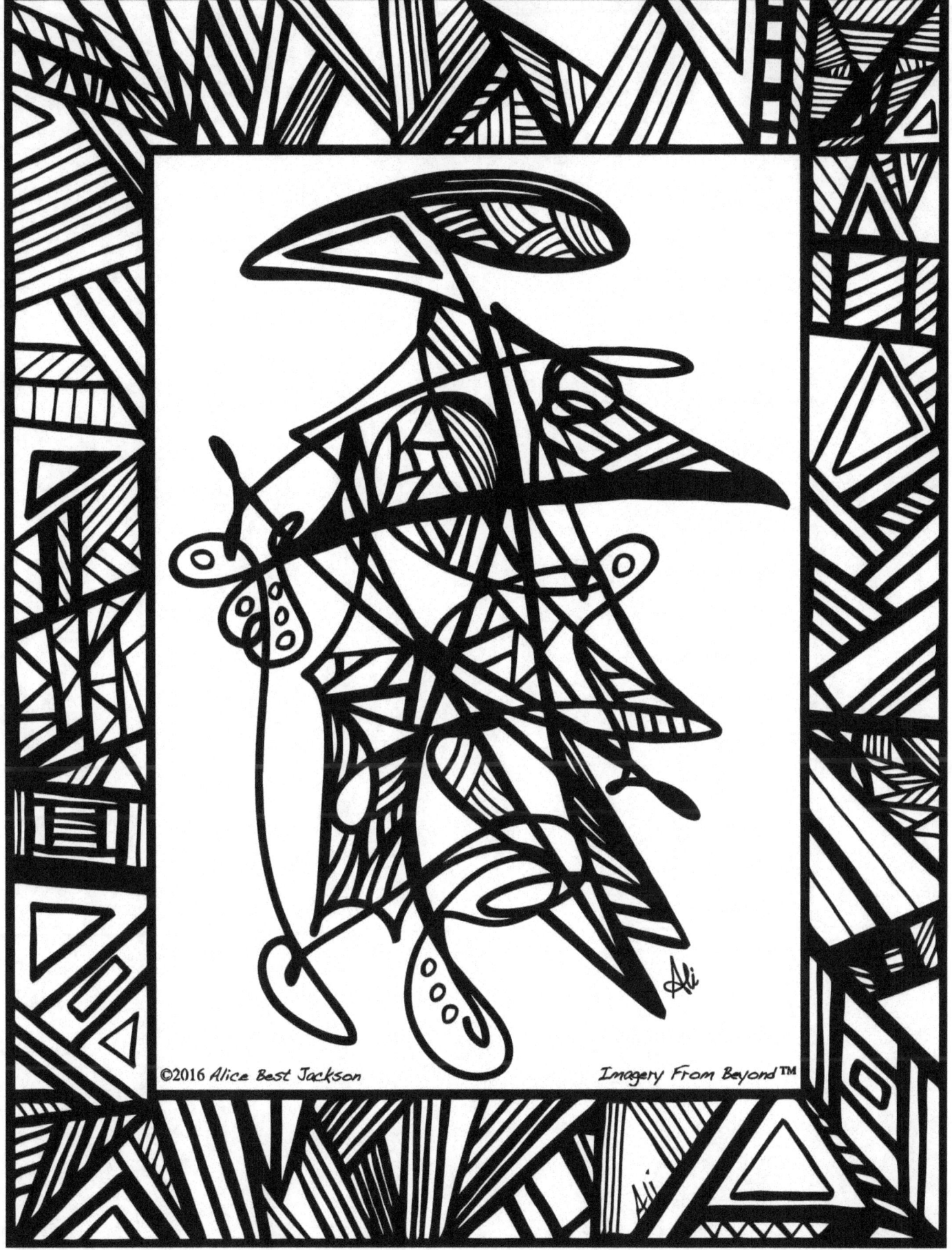

©2016 Alice Best Jackson

Imagery From Beyond™

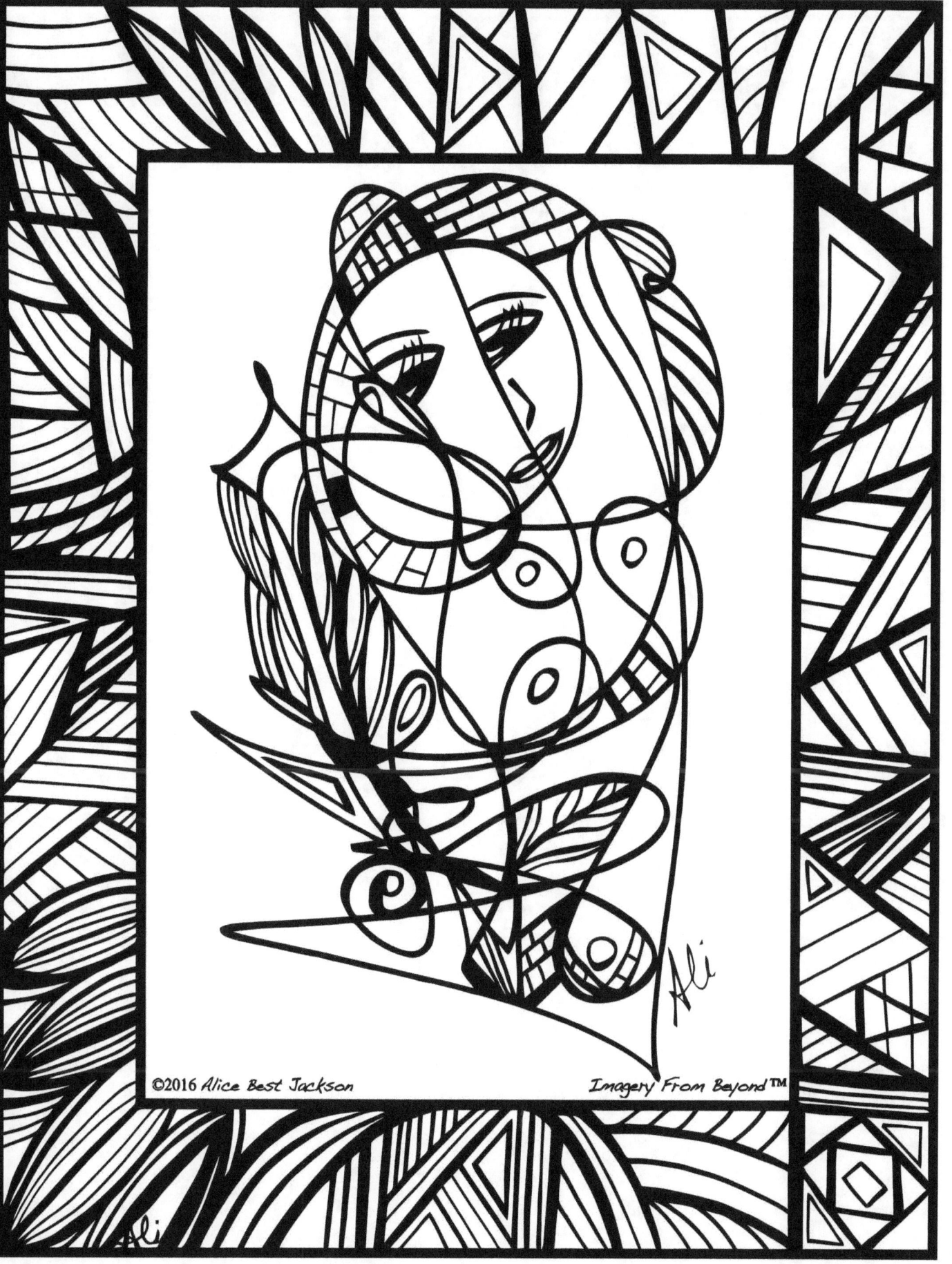

©2016 Alice Best Jackson

Imagery From Beyond™

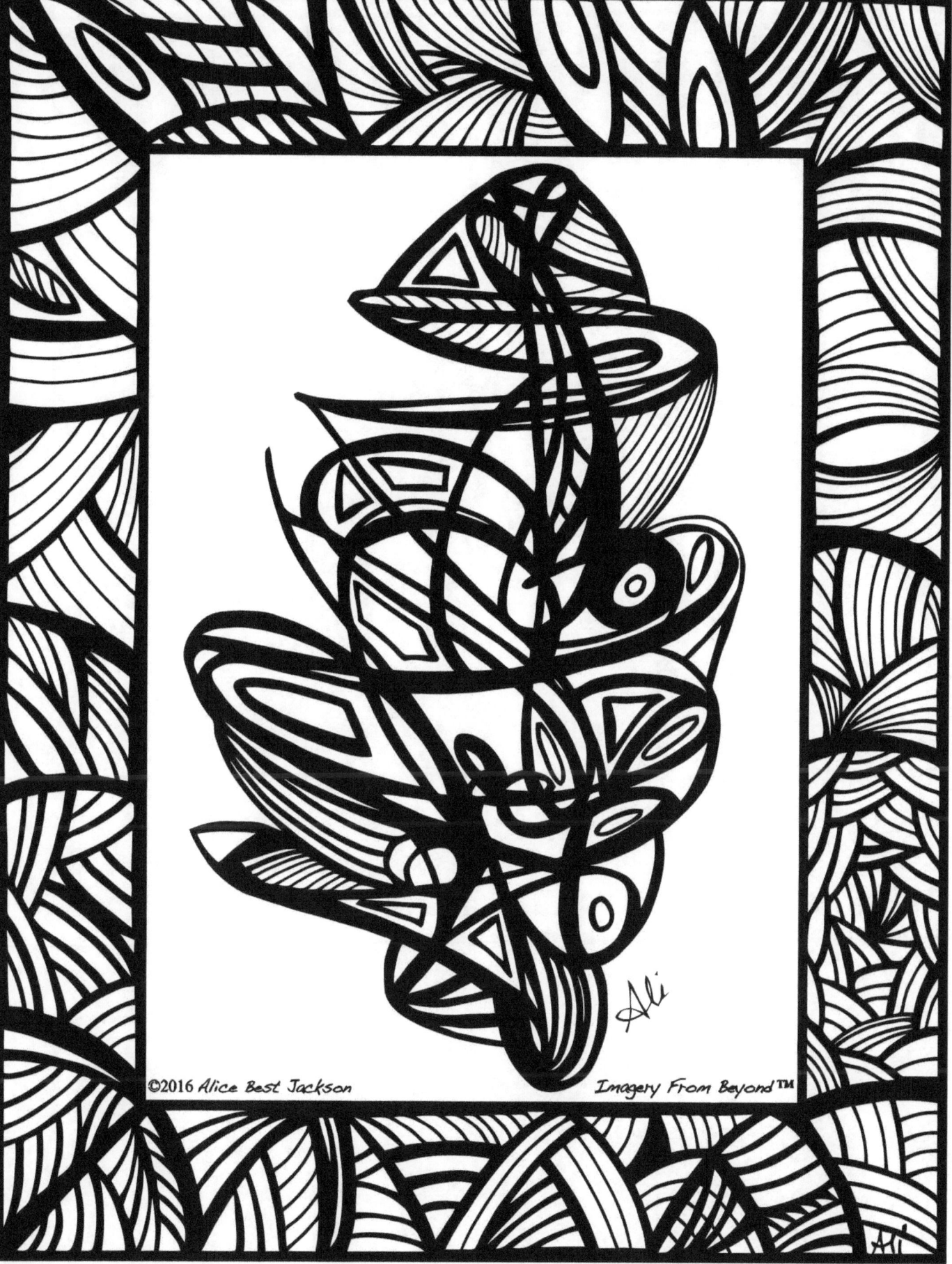

©2016 Alice Best Jackson

Imagery From Beyond™

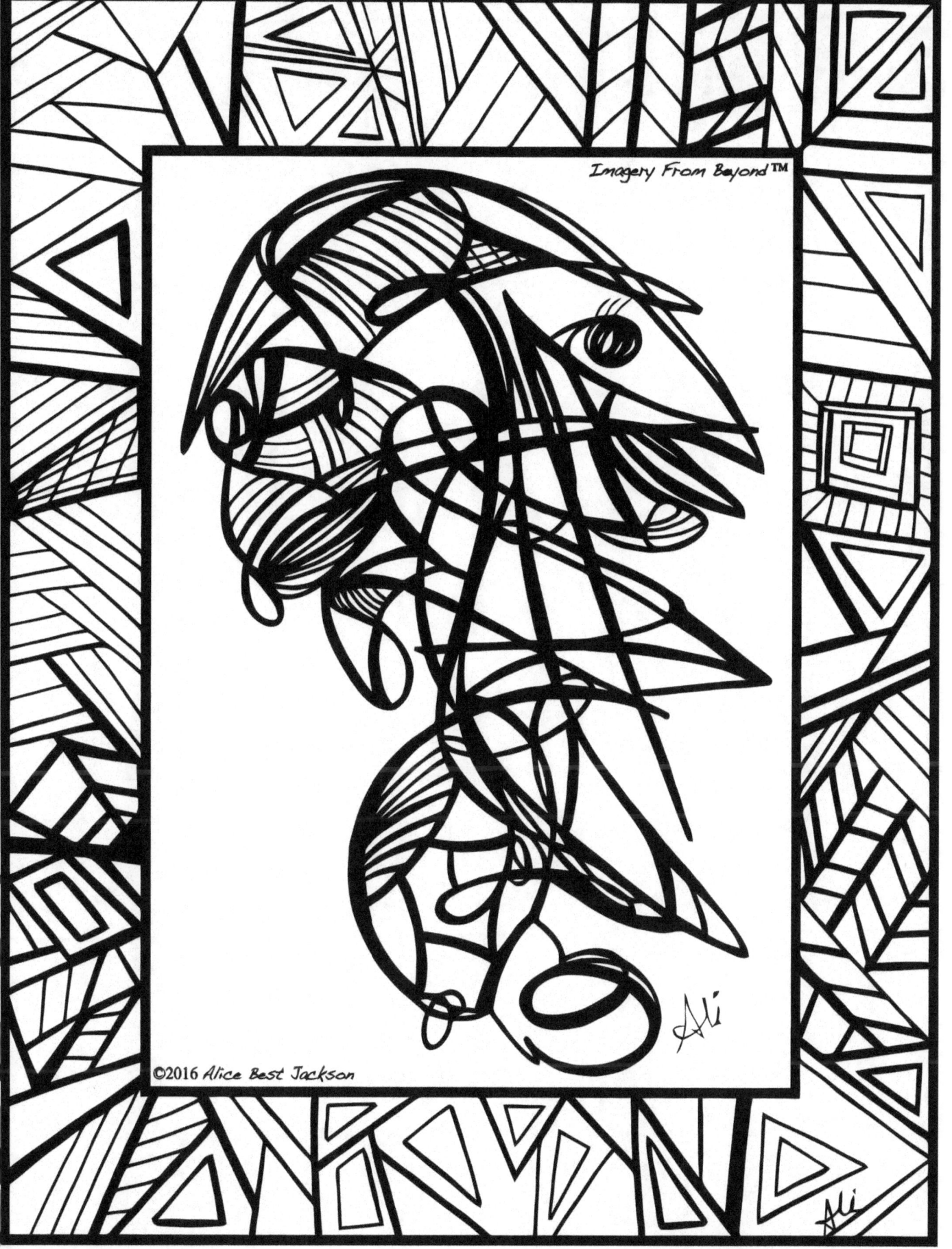

Imagery From Beyond™

©2016 Alice Best Jackson

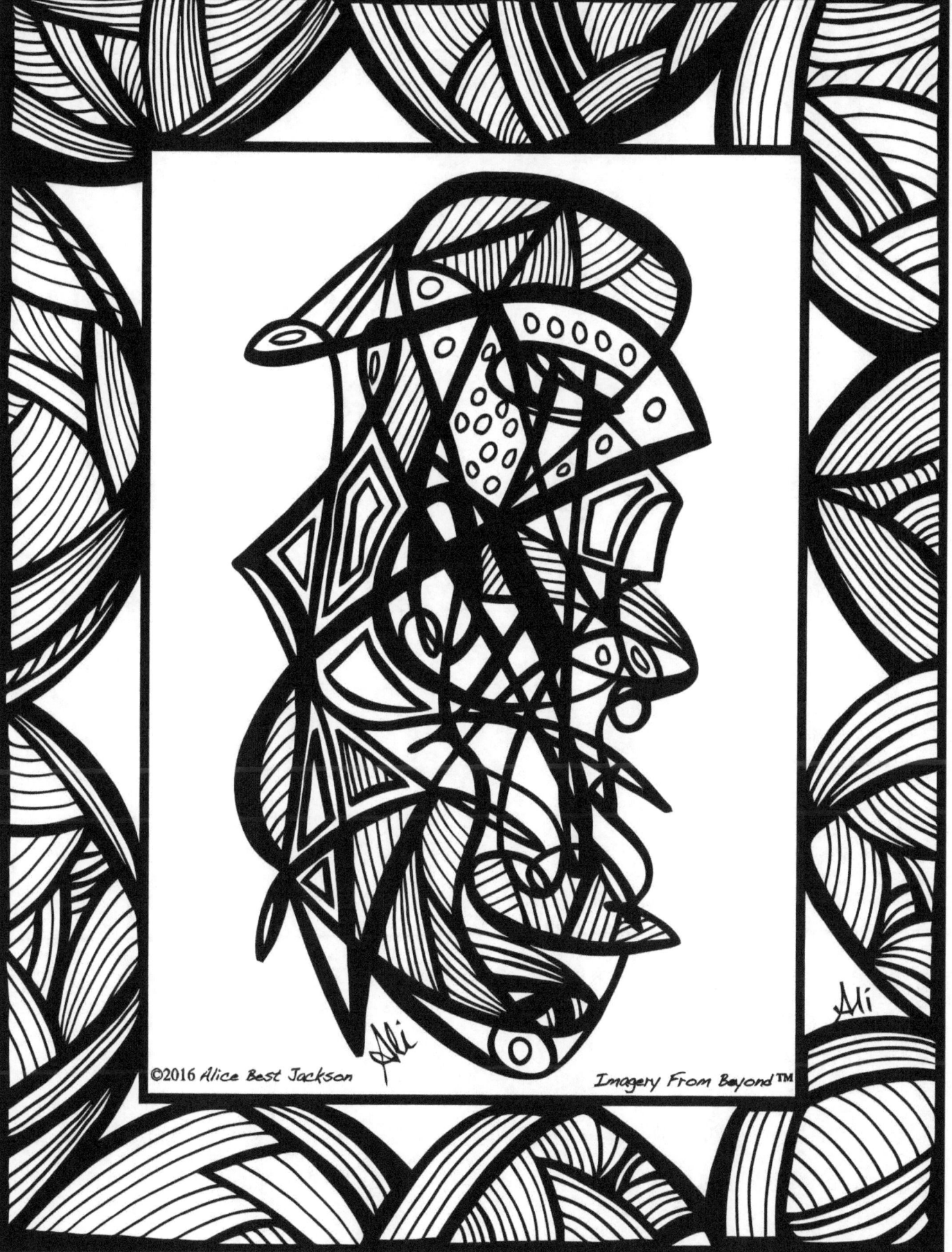

©2016 Alice Best Jackson

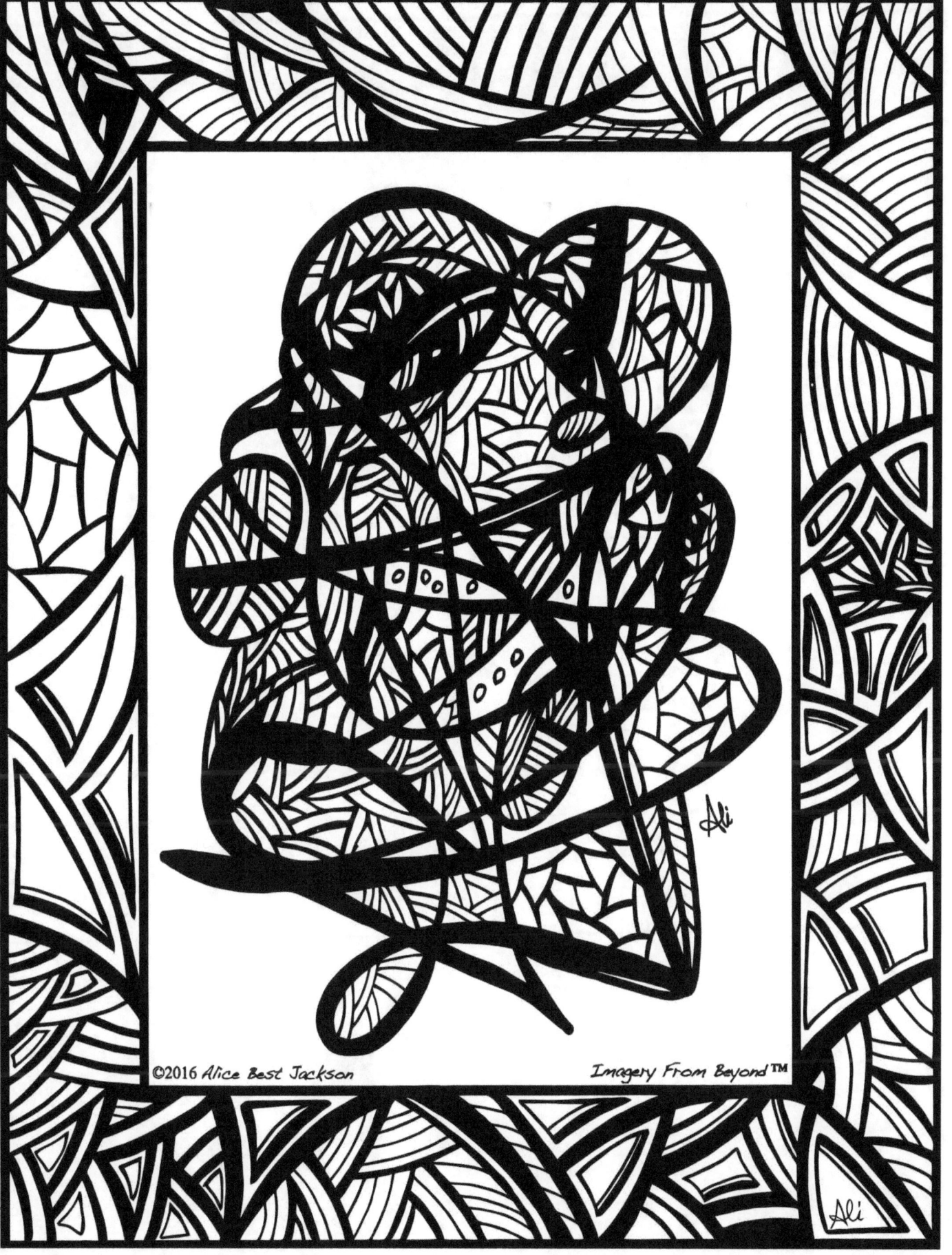

©2016 Alice Best Jackson

Imagery From Beyond™

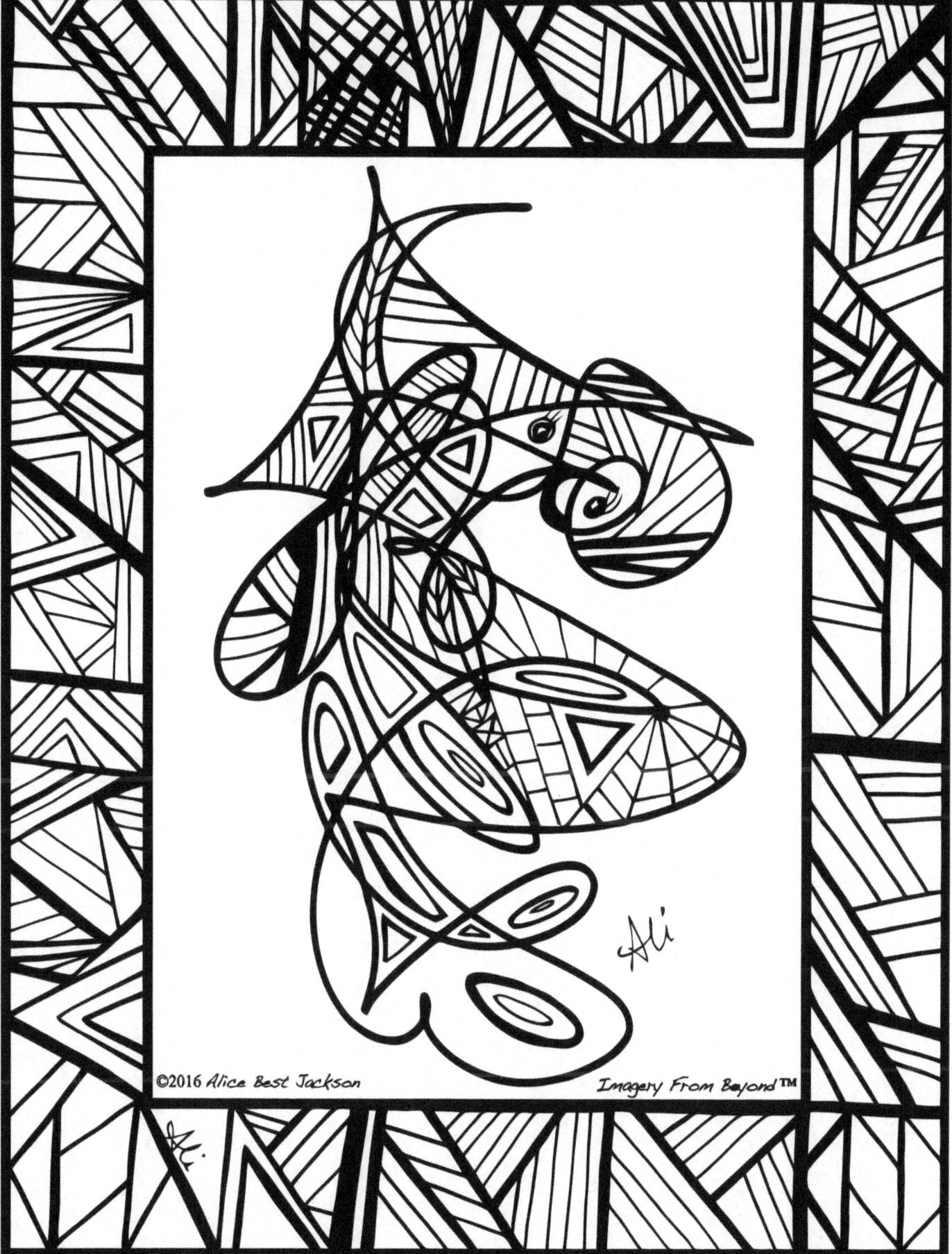

©2016 Alice Best Jackson

Imagery From Beyond™

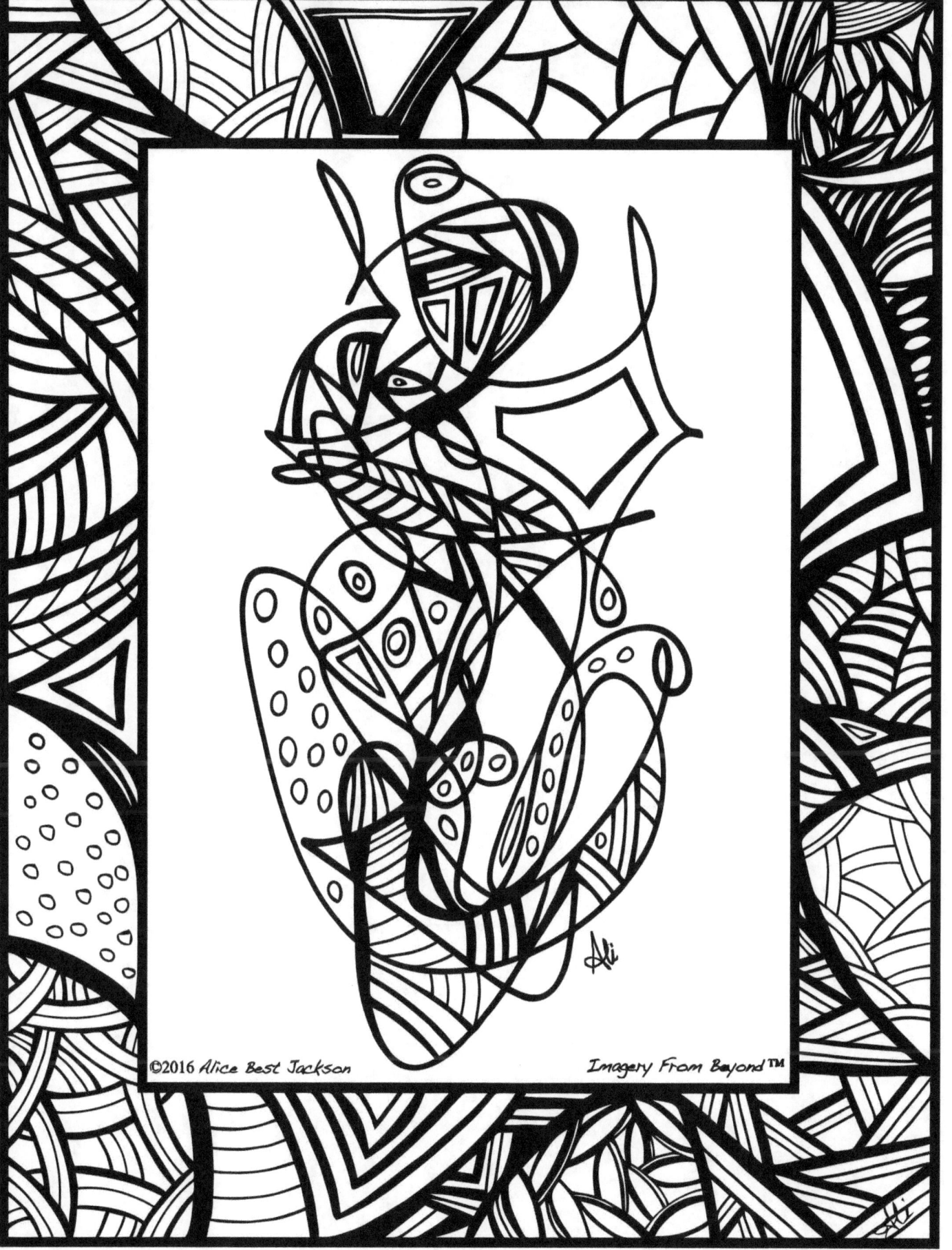

©2016 Alice Best Jackson

Imagery From Beyond™

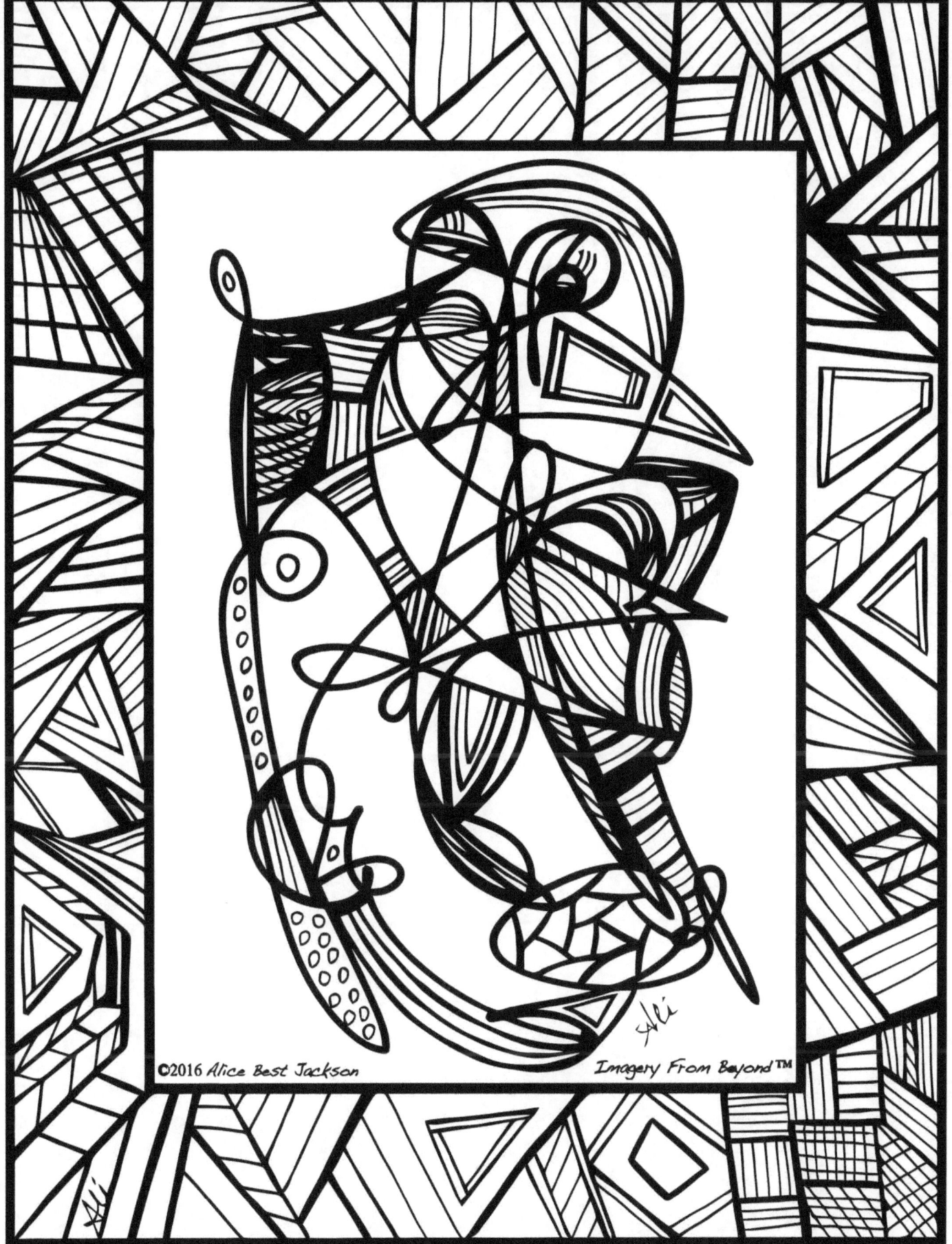

©2016 Alice Best Jackson

Imagery From Beyond™

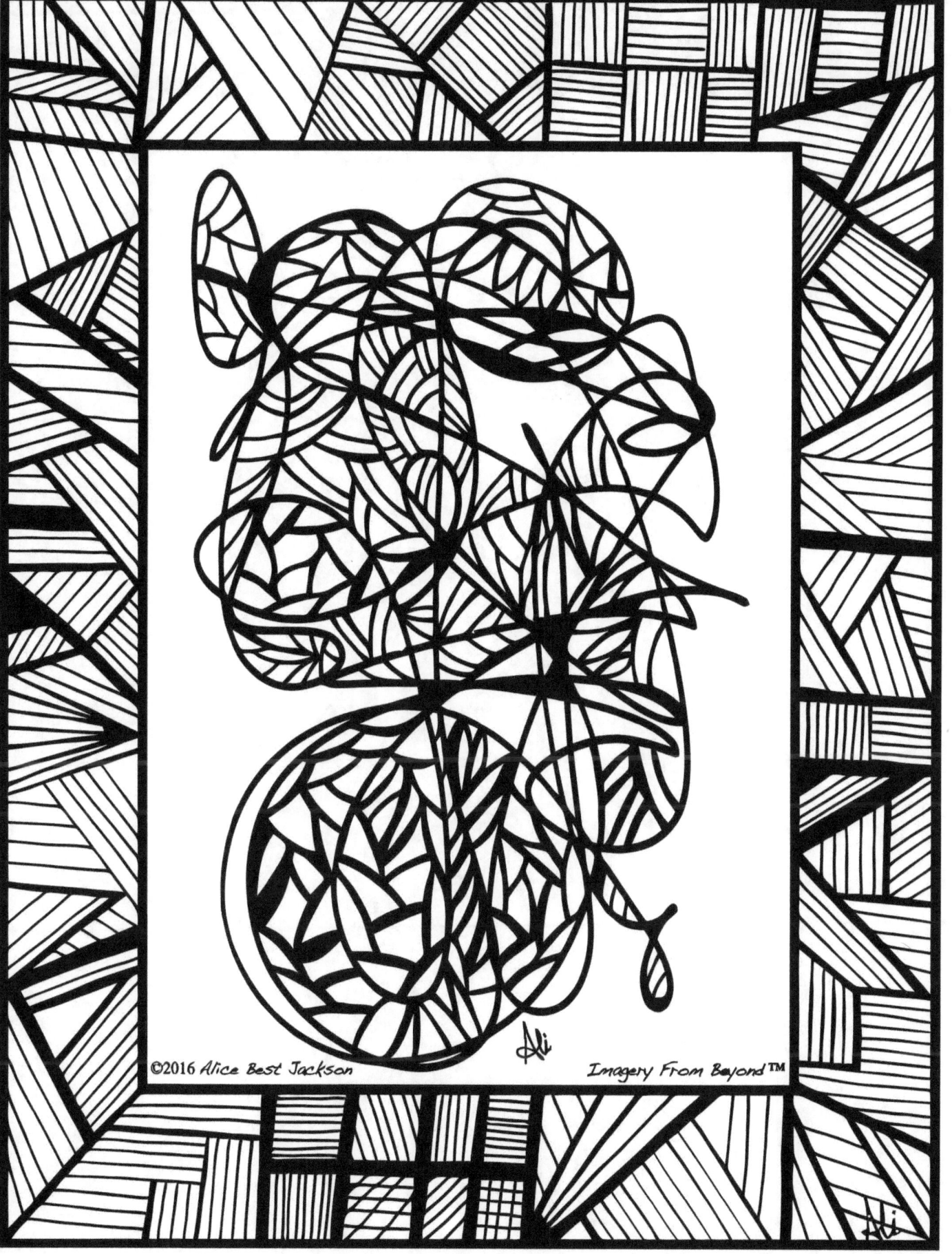

©2016 Alice Best Jackson

Imagery From Beyond™

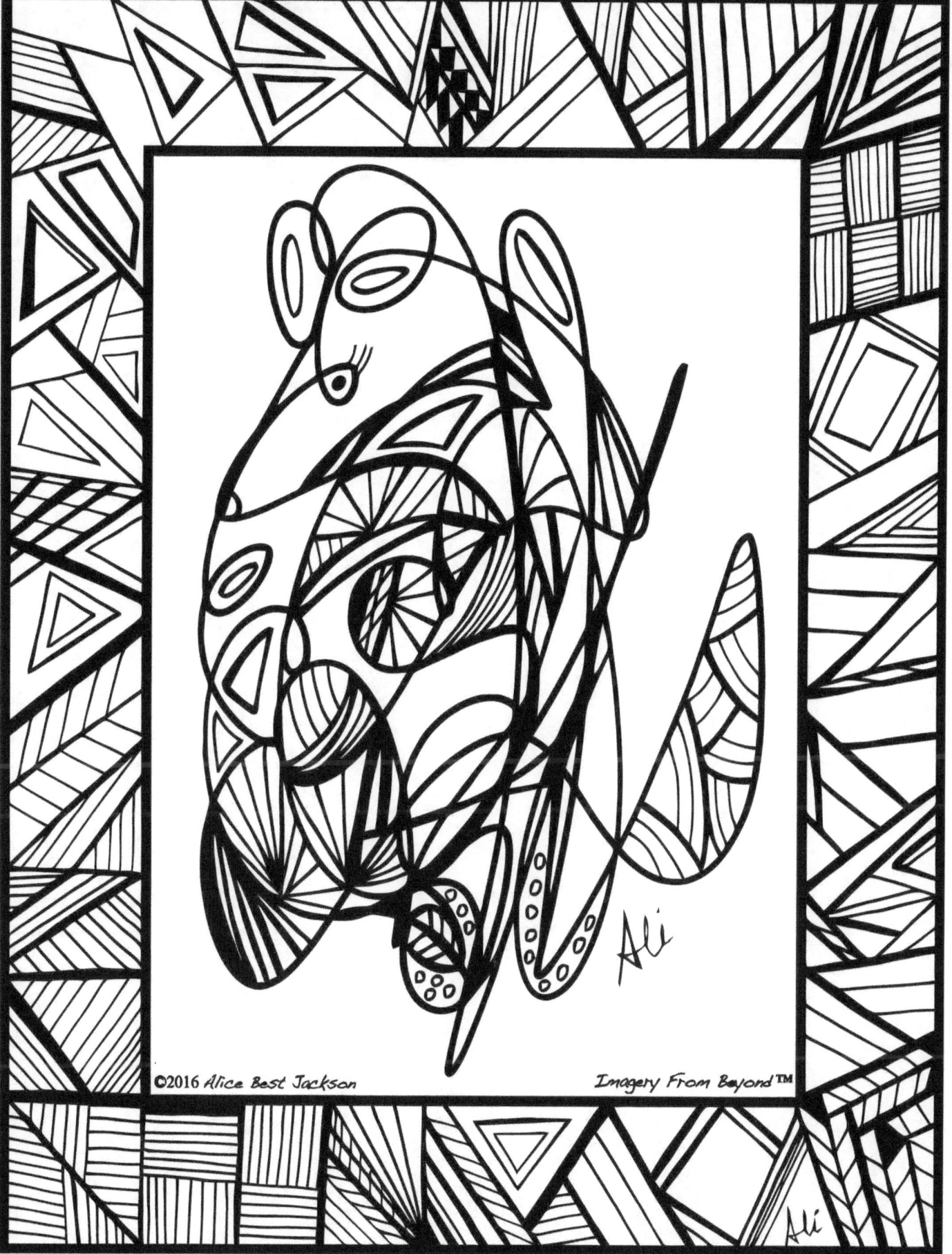

©2016 Alice Best Jackson

Imagery From Beyond™

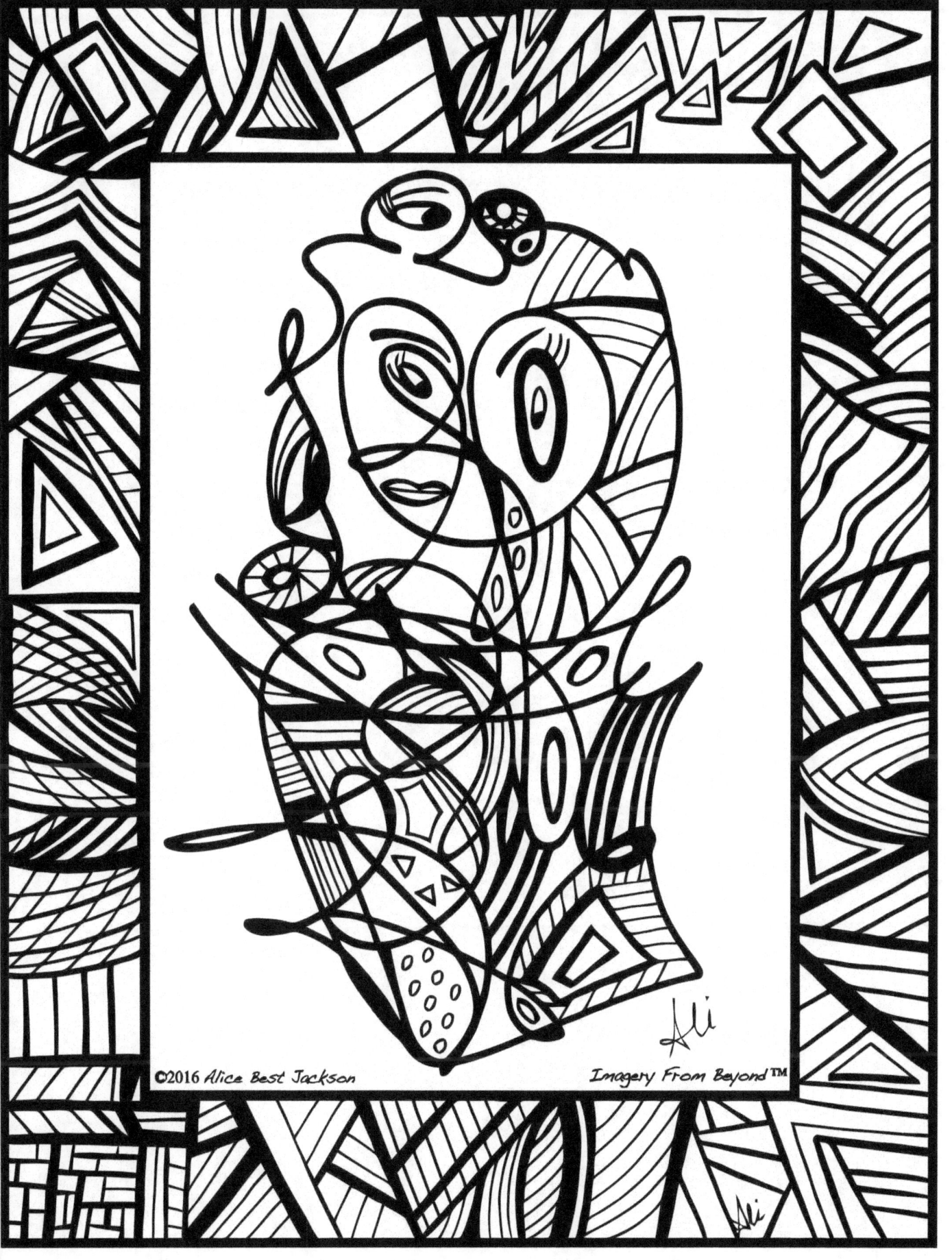

©2016 Alice Best Jackson

Imagery From Beyond™

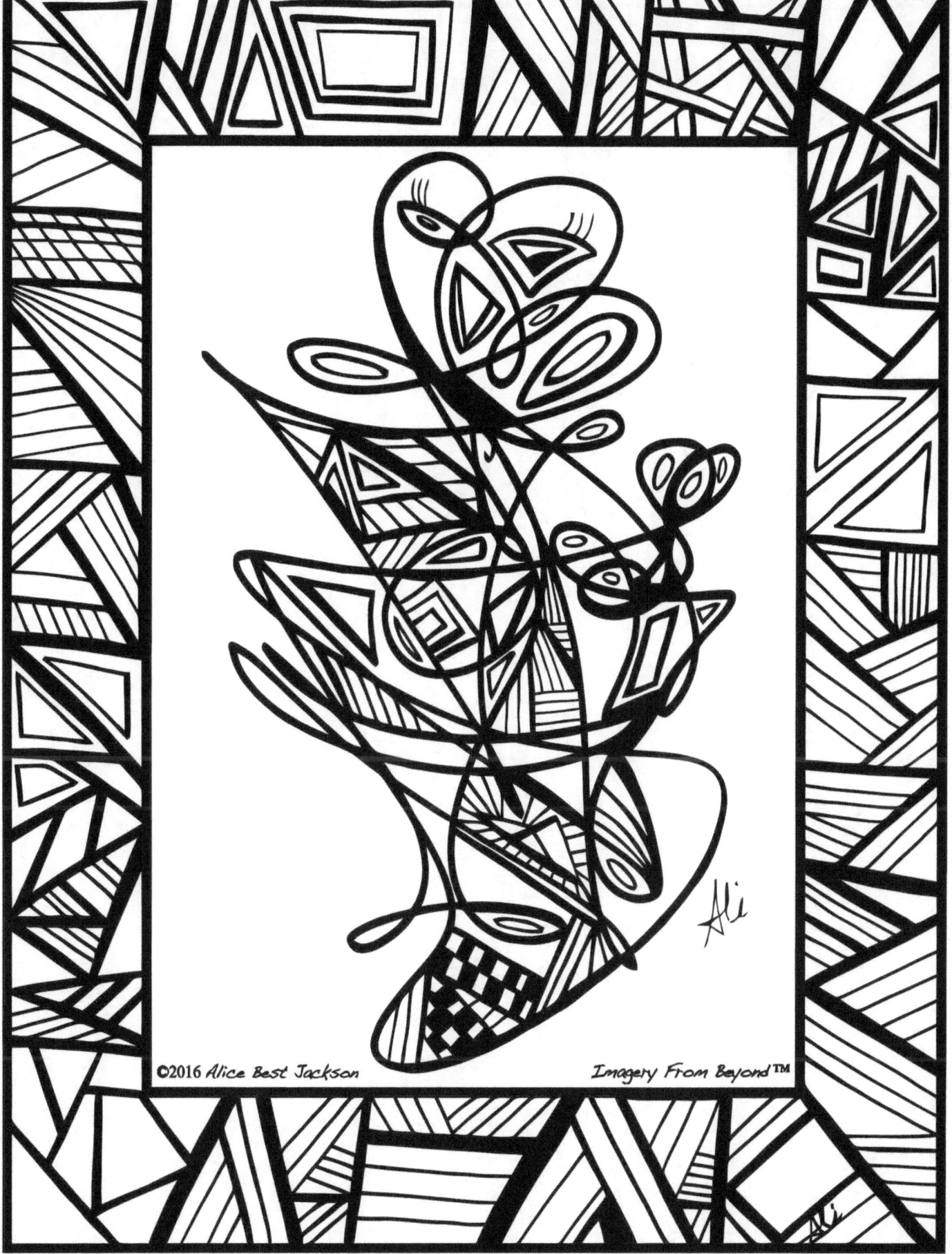

©2016 Alice Best Jackson   Imagery From Beyond™

Meet...
Dennis Jackson & Alice Best Jackson

Dennis Jackson is an internationally acclaimed spiritual medium, author, radio personality, musician, and proud grandpa. Dennis' readings, enhanced by his spirit guides, bring comfort to those whose loved ones have passed over to the other side. Dennis is gifted with the ability to spiritually connect with people and pets both on this side of life and on the other side. Whether in a one-on-one reading or group event, or via television and radio, Dennis' gift of enabling spiritual communication has provided thousands of people with emotional relief, clarity, and direction. His gift consistently brings forth the message that life is continuous and the ones we love remain with us in spirit form. Raised in Washington State, his alter-ego is a local rock star, and he plays lead guitar in his classic rock and cover band, **North by Northwest Band**. They play venues in the greater Seattle area and all around the Pacific Northwest. **www.nxnwband.com**

Alice Best Jackson is a recovering divorce lawyer, native of South Florida, author, intuitive abstract artist, and proud grandma. As the creator of ***Intuitive Art by Ali Designs,*** a method of automatic drawing used during private readings and ***Messages from Beyond*®** events, Alice's ***Art by Ali*™** is featured in ***Imagery From Beyond*™ a Messages From Beyond® Coloring Book** series. Alice has used automatic writing for her personal spiritual growth since 1982, and was surprised and delighted when it evolved into intuitive abstract art in 2001. During her legal career in South Florida (1977-1999), which she began as a legal secretary and paralegal, Alice was a former assistant state attorney under Janet Reno's tenure, owned and managed a successful private practice in family law, and also presided as a traffic court magistrate in Miami-Dade County. She and Dennis relocated to the Seattle area in 1999 to be near family, and to experience their next great adventure!

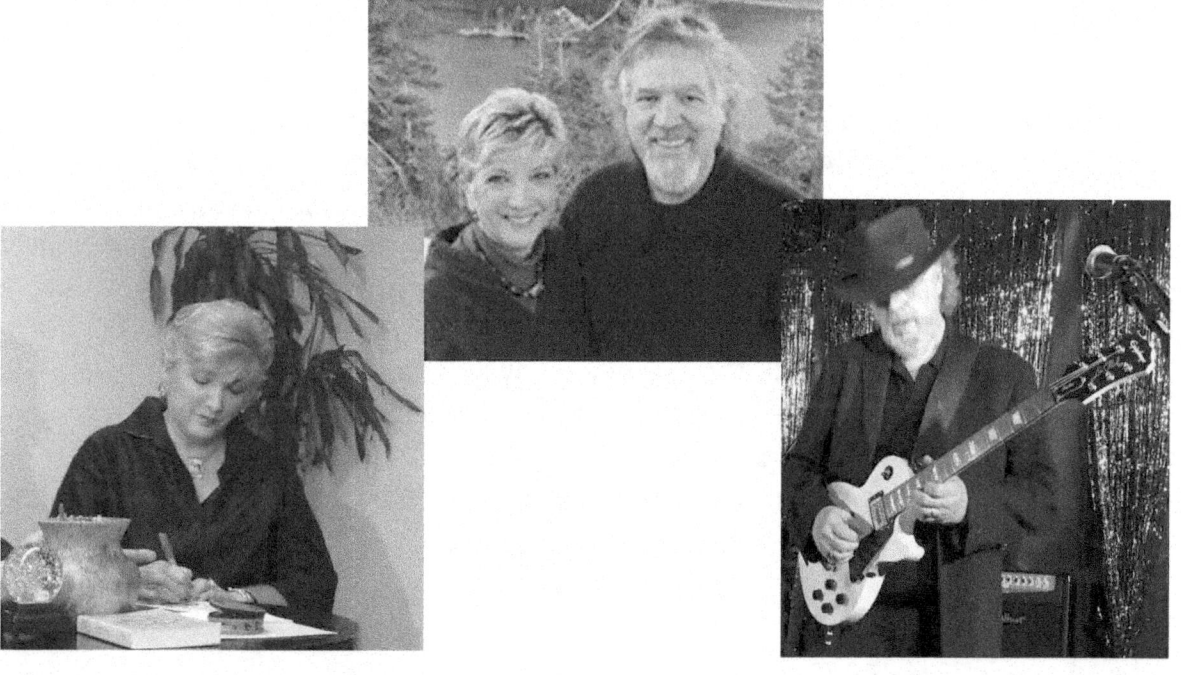

Dennis and Alice are co-hosts of the popular Internet radio show *Messages from Beyond®*, and are frequent radio and TV guests on local stations all across the United States. Their national TV appearances include five segments on *Access Hollywood*. They are considered experts on the subject of Twin Souls and relationships, as well as helping people heal after losing a loved one. **Dennis and Alice's *Messages from Beyond®*** events help participants move through their grief and experience comfort through messages received from loved ones on the other side.

Dennis and Alice have traveled around the U.S. presenting classes and workshops on relationships, spirituality, dream analysis, and developing intuitive pathways, and plan to do more in the future. As **Twin Soul Spiritual Mediums, Dennis and Alice** find it rewarding to work with people and assist them in tapping into their own natural psychic abilities, providing them with the tools to recognize and solve their own issues, thus enabling participants to regain control and power over their own lives. They have produced a variety of meditations which are available through their website as MP3s or CDs.
www.MessagesFromBeyond.com

In addition to their coloring book series, they are co-authors of the books:
Together Again: Twin Souls Reunite in Love and Life,
and ***Life is an Illusion: Loving Messages from Beyond*** (to be published in 2016). Maintaining a five-star rating on **Amazon.com** and **bn.com**, ***Together Again*** has been endorsed by best selling authors, *Larry King, James Redfield*, and *Alan Cohen*.

Thank you for choosing our book to be a part of your creative process.

We hope you enjoyed your experiences while coloring these pages. We'd love to hear from you, and welcome all comments, compliments, aha moments, as well as your critiques and suggestions for future books in our series. After you've created your specially colored images, if you'd like to share your finished ***Art by Ali™*** colored design with others, please upload a copy to our fan page on **Facebook** at **www.facebook.com/ImageryFromBeyond**. We may also share some of your finished art on our website. Send us emails, too! Tell us what images you see and how you felt while coloring. That's what this is all about...art therapy, stress reduction, imagery, comfort, and healing for all. There is never any judgment on coloring... each piece is unique and beautiful as the colors bring them to life. We hope you also enjoyed your play date with your inner child. Come back often, happy coloring, and enjoy your...
Imagery From Beyond™.

Dennis and Alice

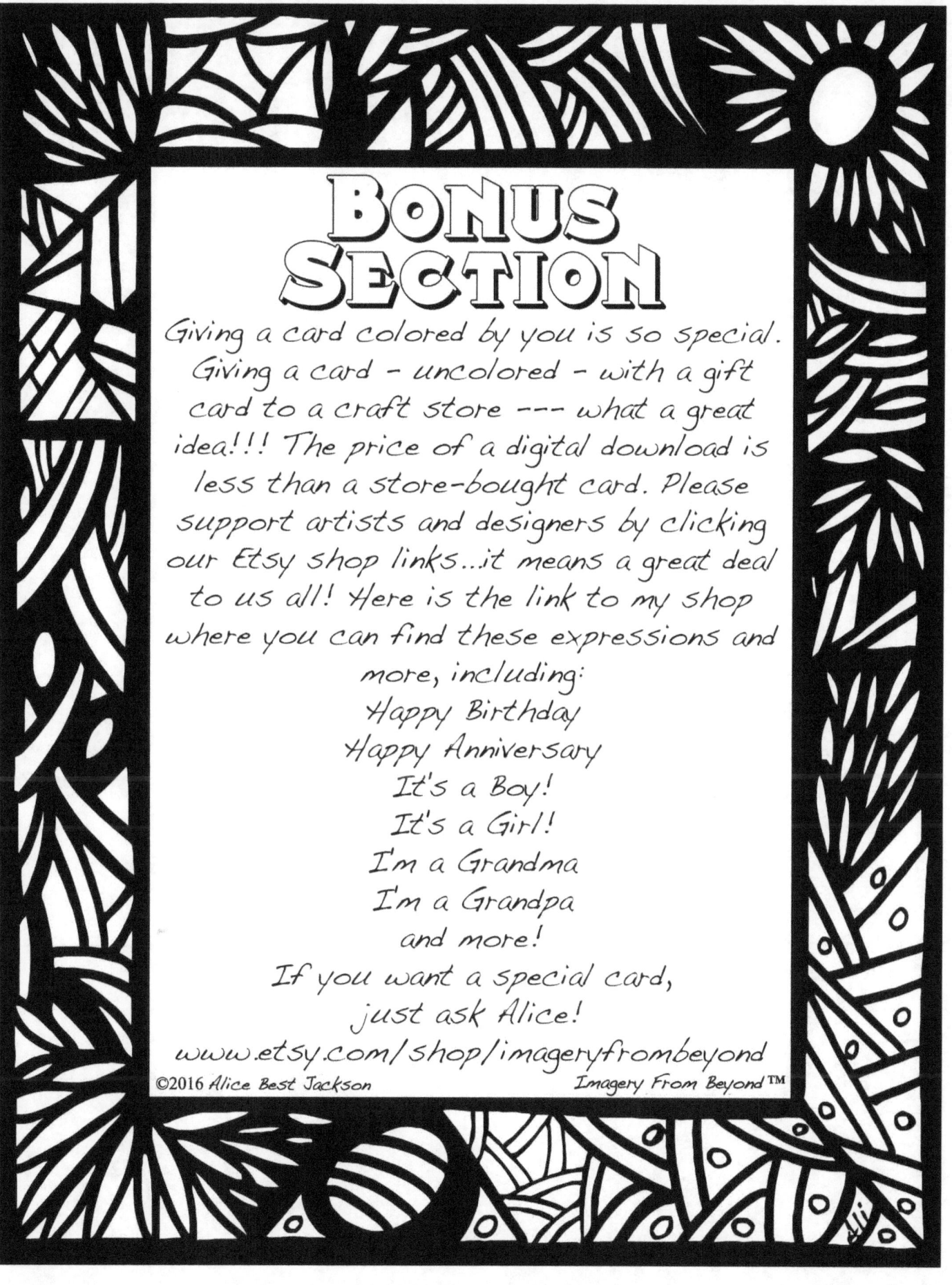

BONUS SECTION

Giving a card colored by you is so special. Giving a card - uncolored - with a gift card to a craft store --- what a great idea!!! The price of a digital download is less than a store-bought card. Please support artists and designers by clicking our Etsy shop links...it means a great deal to us all! Here is the link to my shop where you can find these expressions and more, including:

Happy Birthday

Happy Anniversary

It's a Boy!

It's a Girl!

I'm a Grandma

I'm a Grandpa

and more!

If you want a special card, just ask Alice!

www.etsy.com/shop/imageryfrombeyond

Imagery From Beyond™

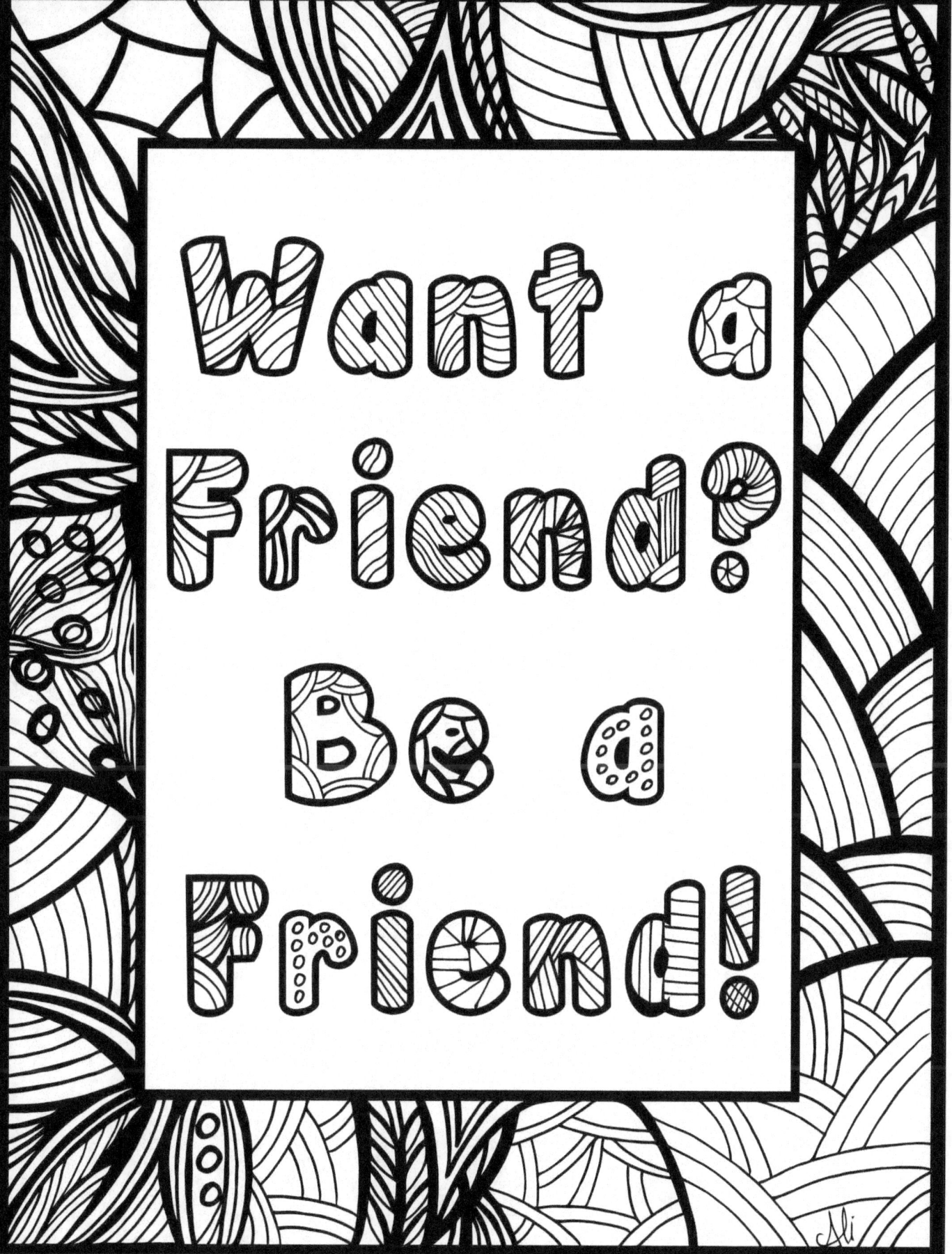

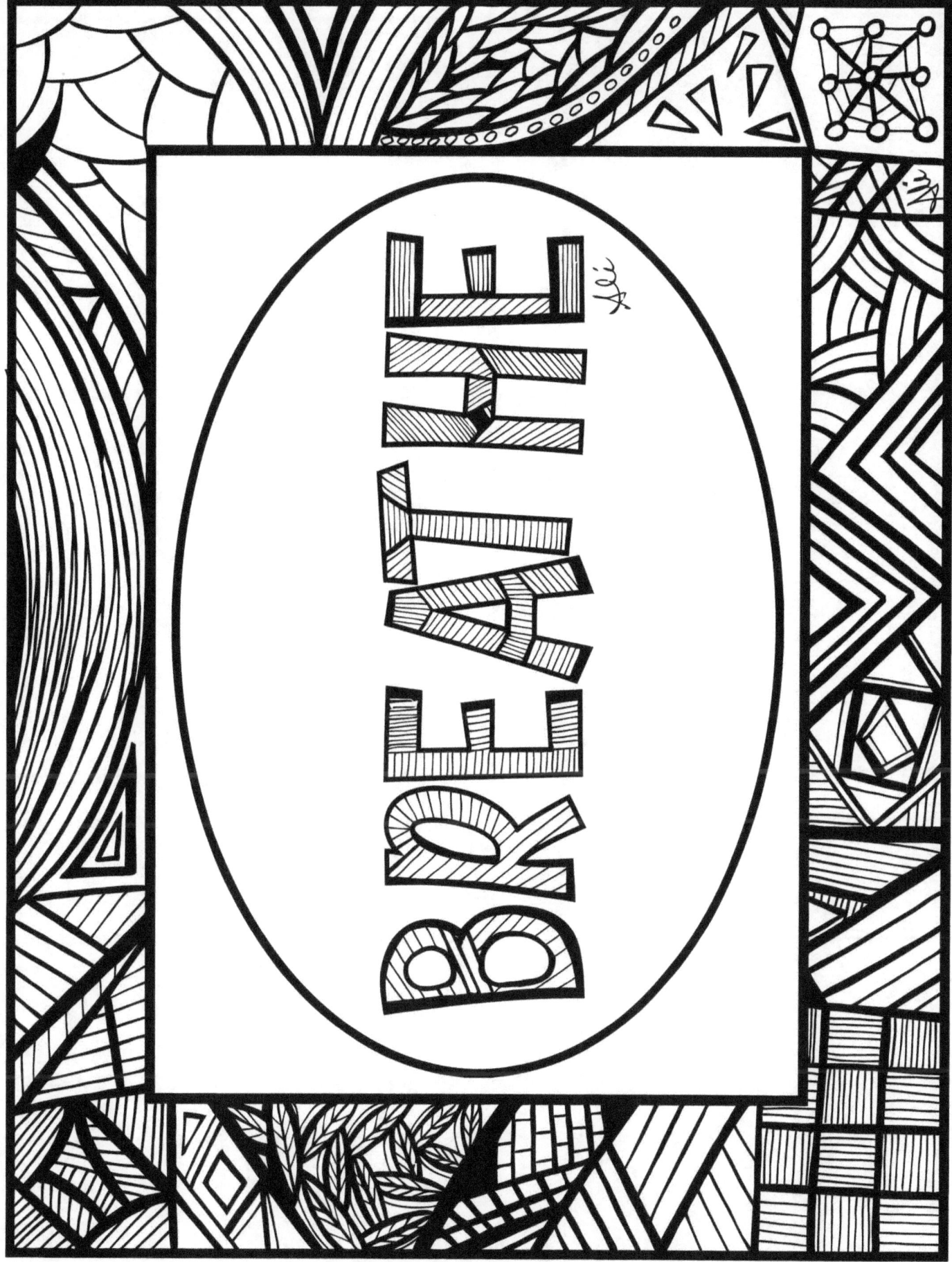

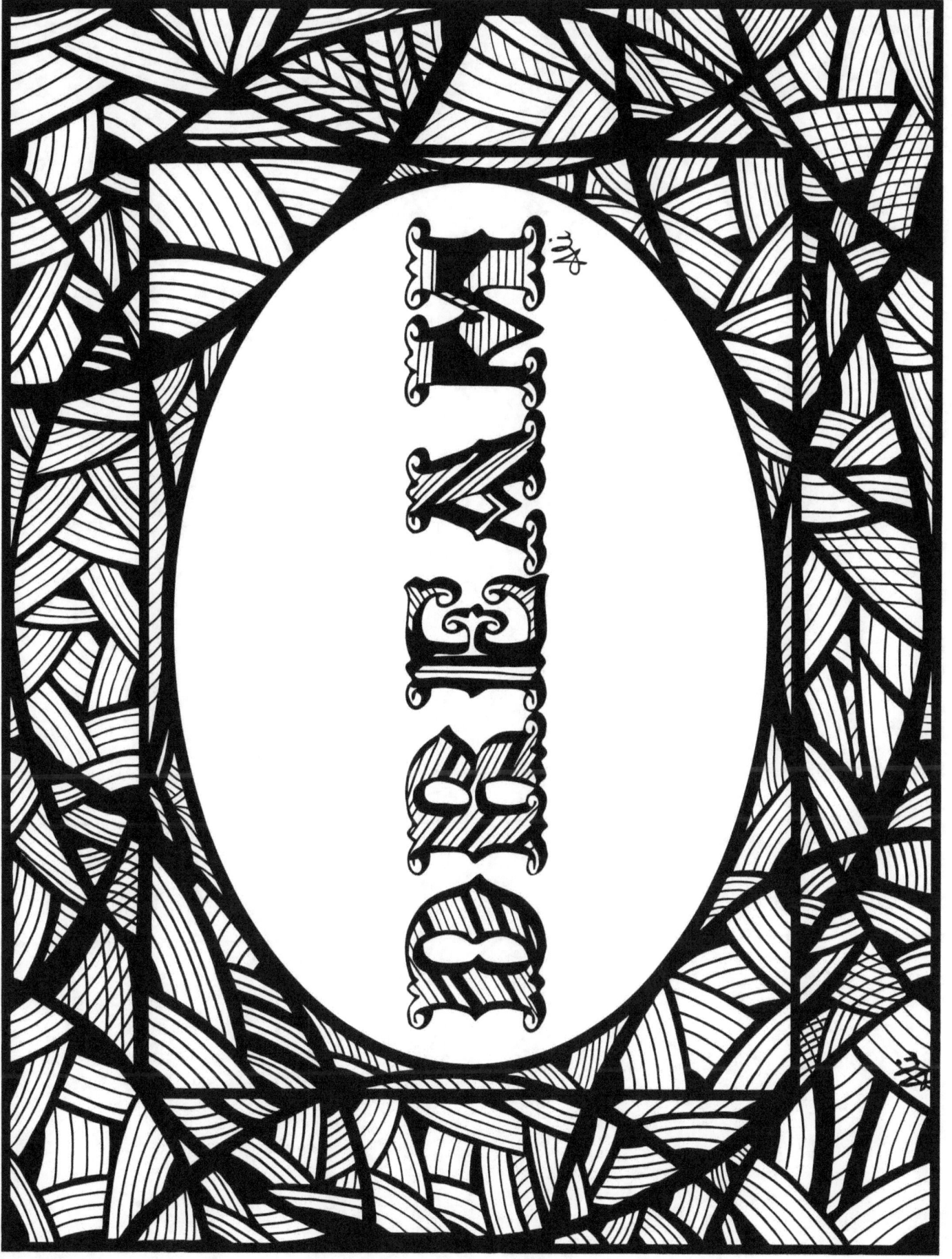

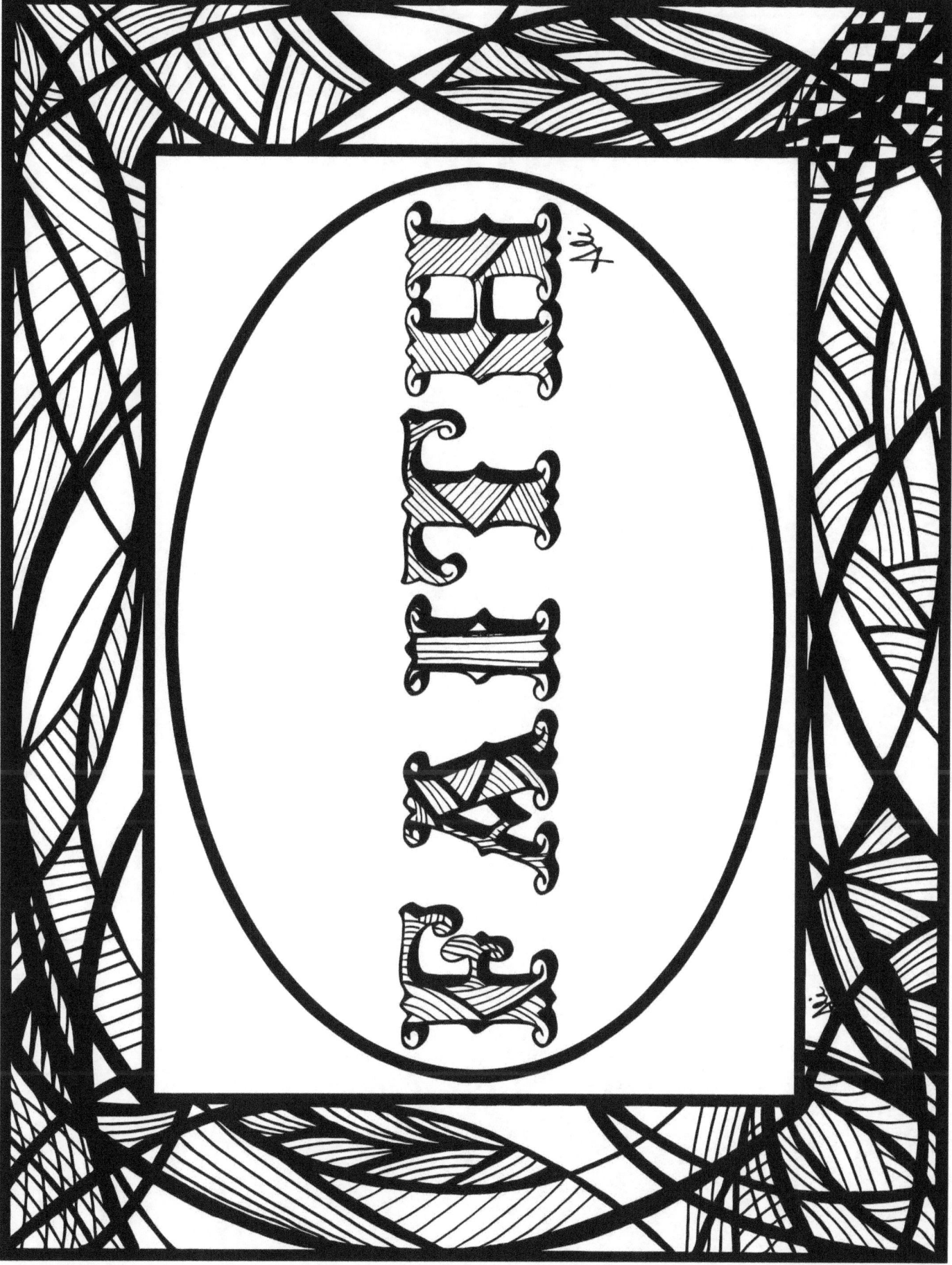

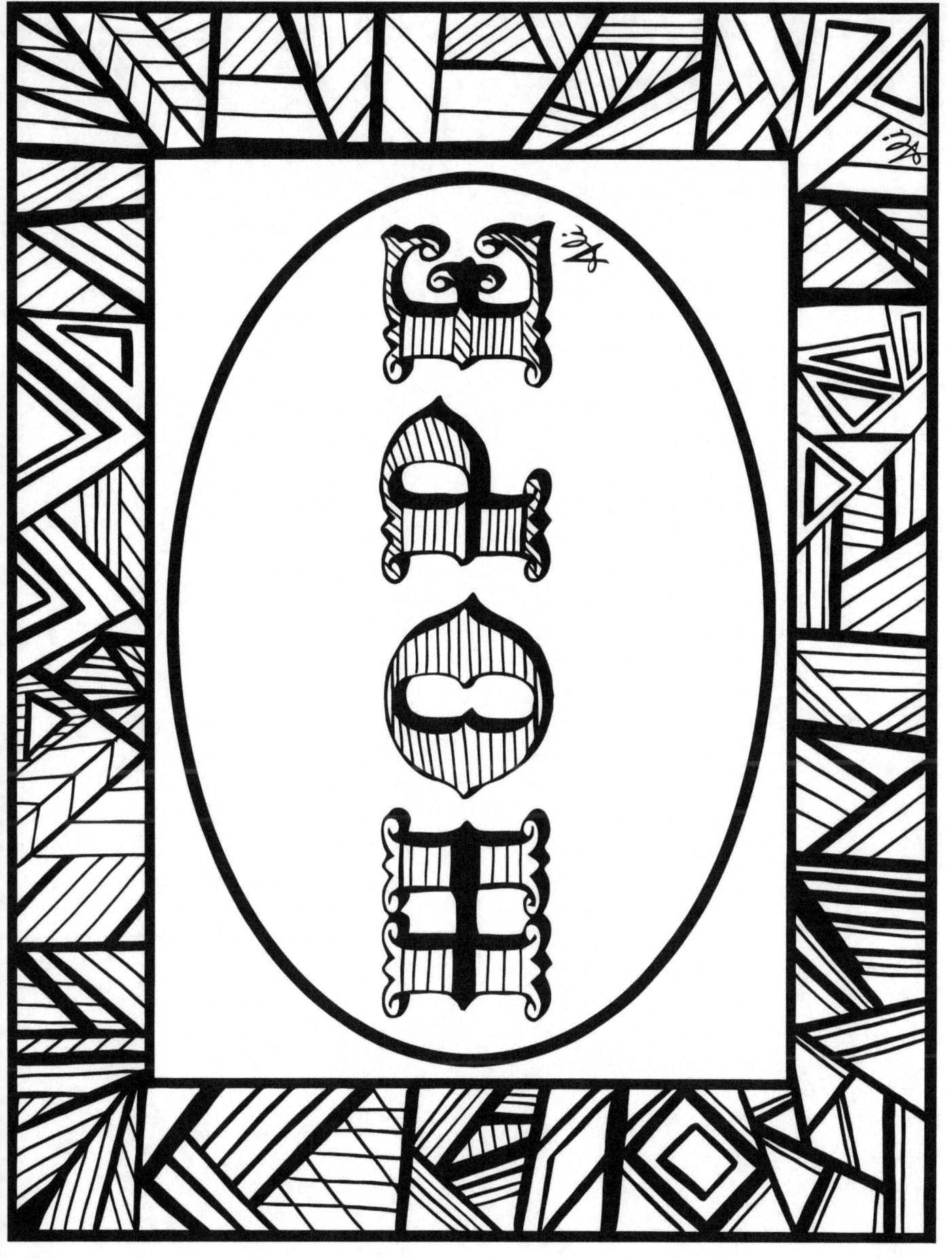

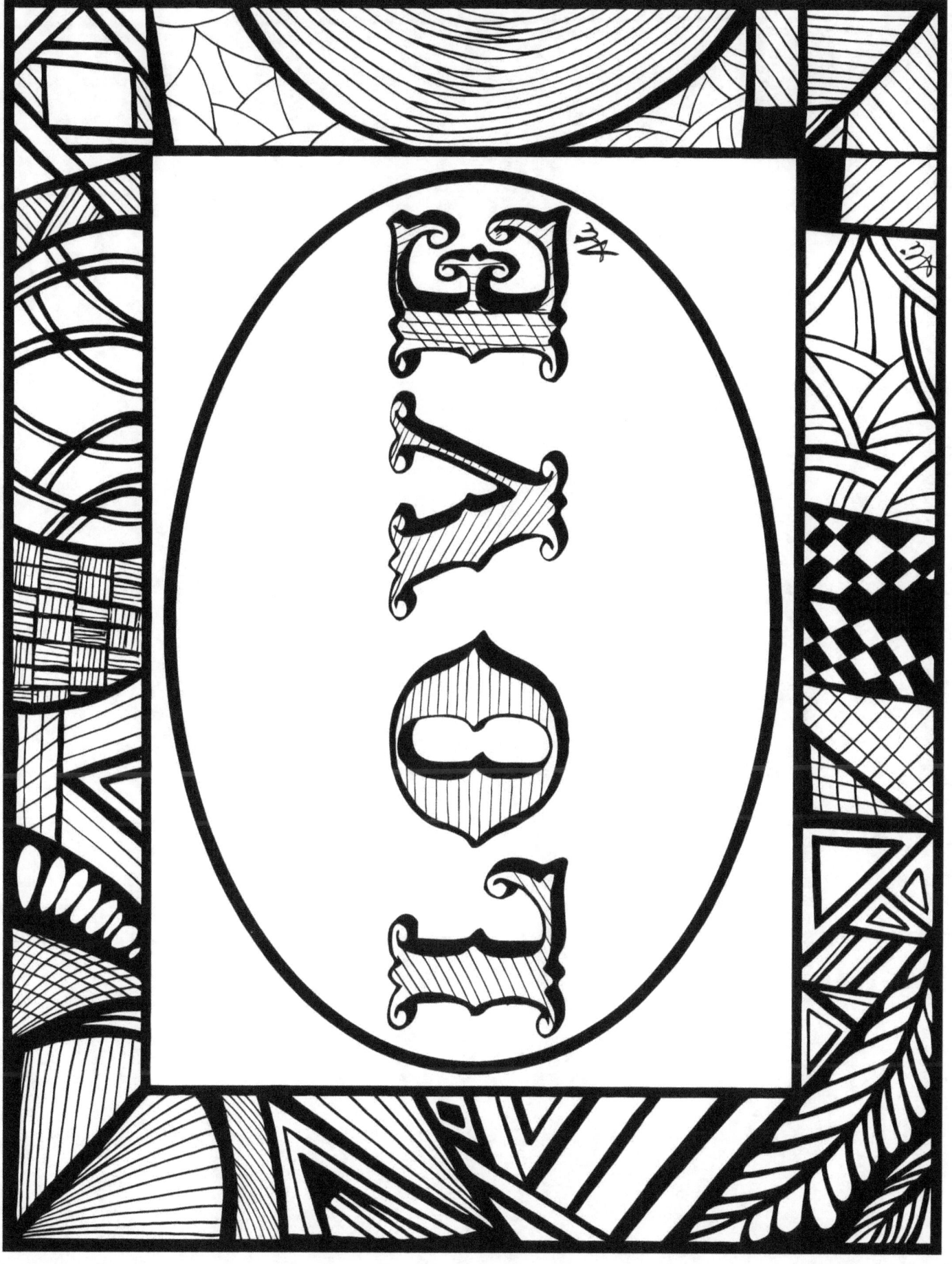

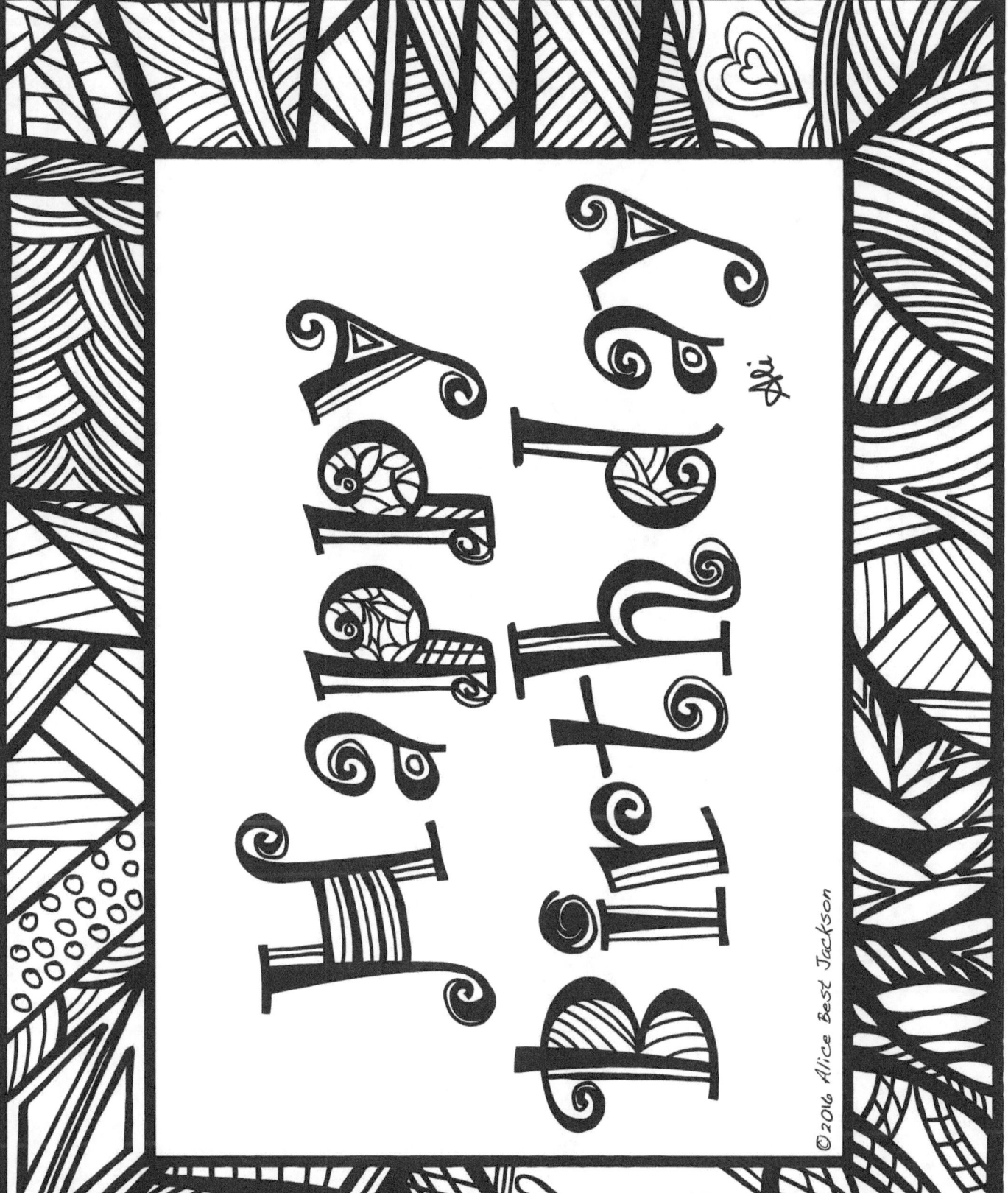

© 2016 Alice Best Jackson

©2016 Alice Best Jackson

Imagery From Beyond™

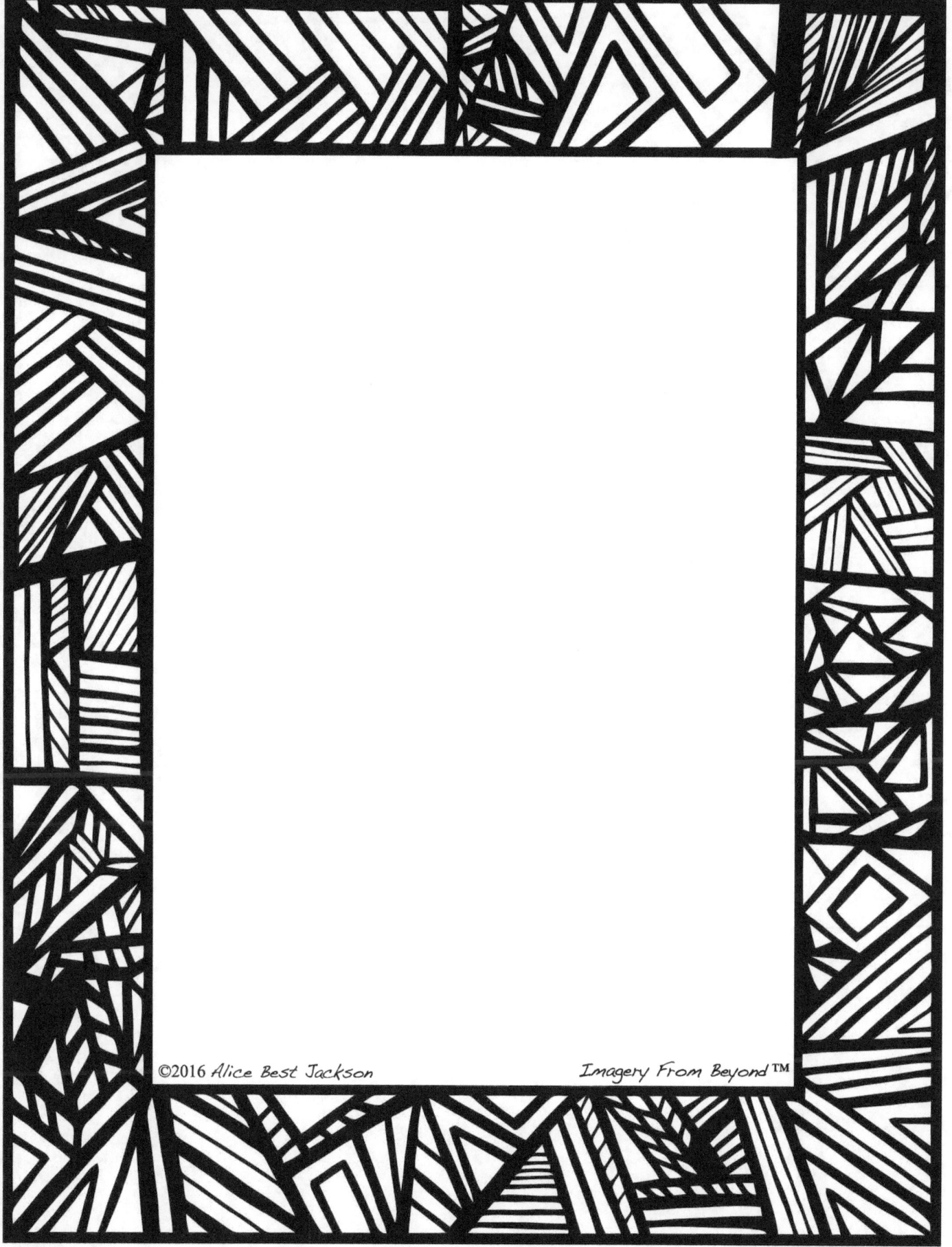

©2016 Alice Best Jackson

Imagery From Beyond™

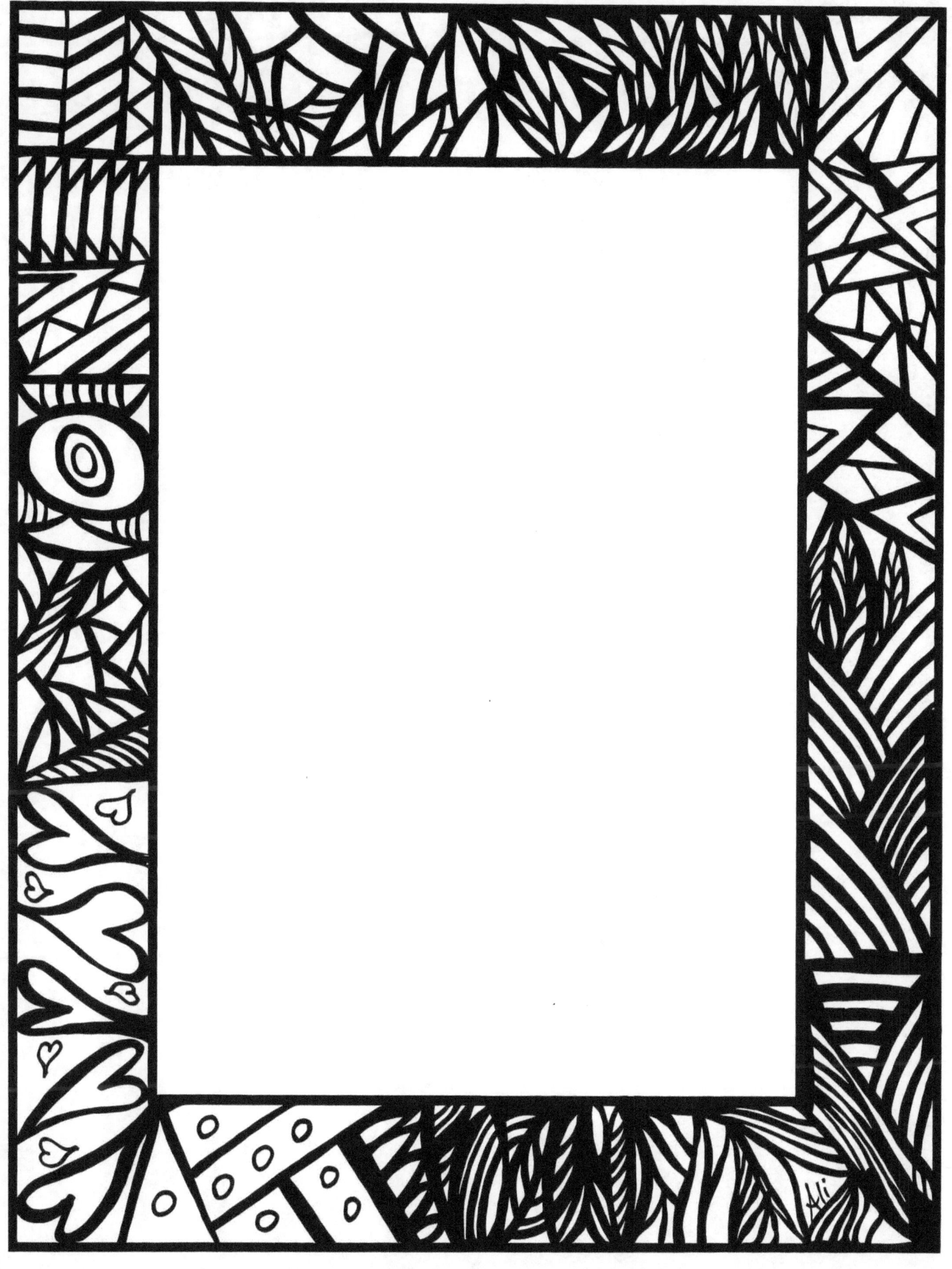

Let's stay in touch...
Like us? Please let us know, and follow us online.
Love us? Let others know, too!

Now that you've chosen **Imagery From Beyond™**, we'd love to see how you bring **Art by Ali™** designs to life. We invite you to share your colored pages on social media sites, including ours.

Reviews are important!!
Authors and artists are especially appreciative of good reviews. If you enjoy this book, please tell your friends...all of them! And let the world see your coloring by posting online colored pages and reviews at **Amazon.com** and in your coloring groups. If you don't like something, let us know directly so we can consider your comments for future books. **Please remember, we have no control over the paper quality, and are using the best quality available for print on demand coloring books by CreateSpace and Amazon.**

To leave a review, visit:
www.amazon.com/author/alicebestjackson or www.imageryfrombeyond.com
and click on the picture of the book you'd like to review. The link will take you directly to the book's page on **Amazon.com** where you can leave a review (the more stars, the better!!!), and order copies for your friends or send them the link to order their own.

Coloring Team. If you're interested in being a colorist for **Imagery From Beyond™** and perhaps seeing your colored page on a future book cover, send Alice an email or Facebook message and ask how to become a coloring team member.
imageryfrombeyond@yahoo.com

Where to find all our books.
Our author page on Amazon also lists all book titles:
www.amazon.com/author/alicebestjackson

Be the first to know about new books, events, appearances, and FREE pages by joining our newsletter mailing list at: **www.MessagesFromBeyond.com**
While you're at the website, download our FREE 30-minute meditation by Dennis:
F.R.E.D. Finding Relief Eliminating Disease.
Double your relaxation: listen to the meditation while coloring!
You may share the link and meditation with your friends!

Follow Imagery From Beyond™ and Messages From Beyond® online:
www.Facebook.com/ImageryFromBeyond
www.Facebook.com/MessagesFromBeyond
www.Facebook.com/groups/ColoringBookTreasury
www.Twitter.com/mssgsfrombeyond @mssgsfrombeyond
www.instagram.com/denalijackson
www.Etsy.com/shop/ImageryFromBeyond

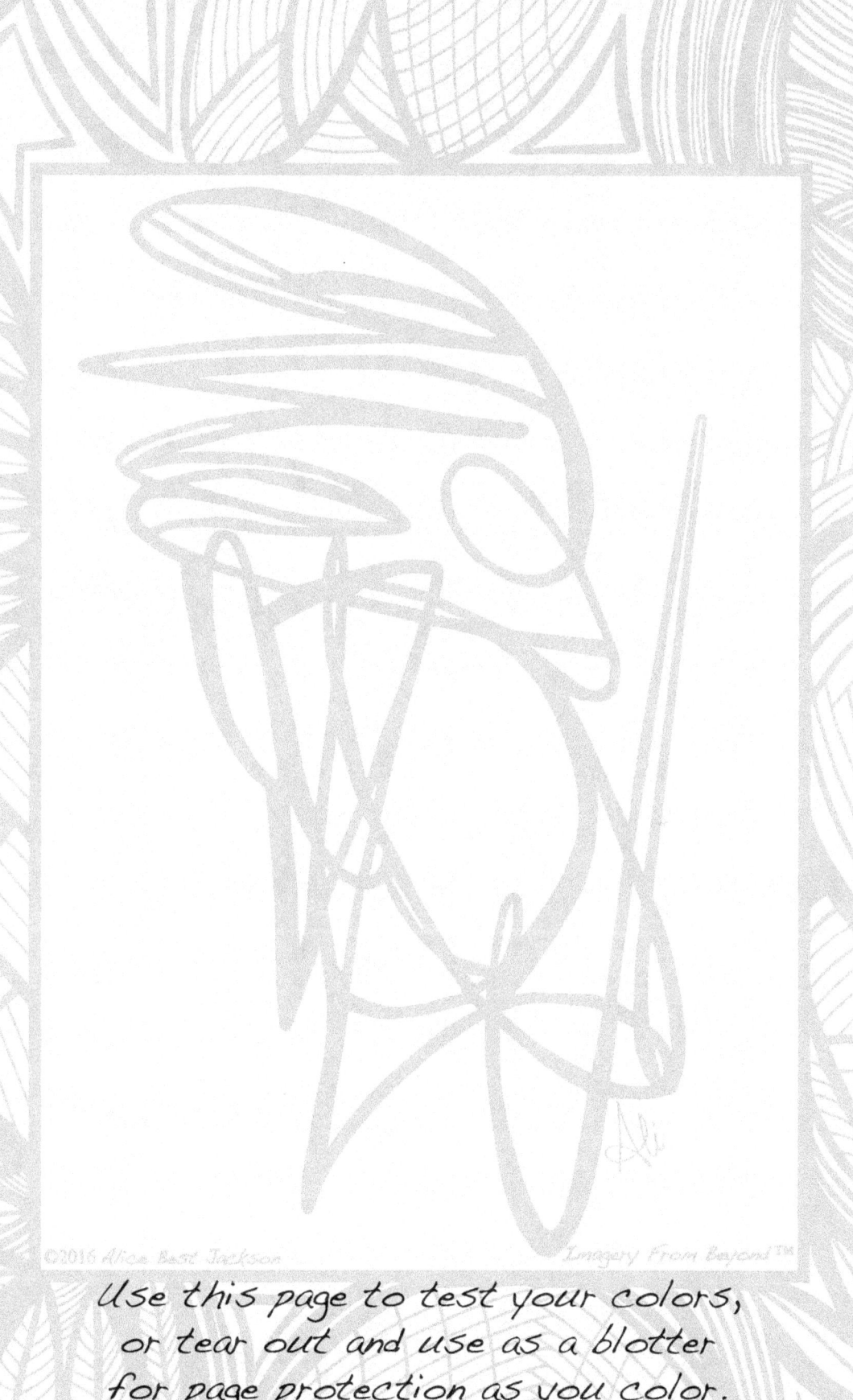

©2016 Alice Bast Jackson   Imagery From Beyond™

Use this page to test your colors,
or tear out and use as a blotter
for page protection as you color.

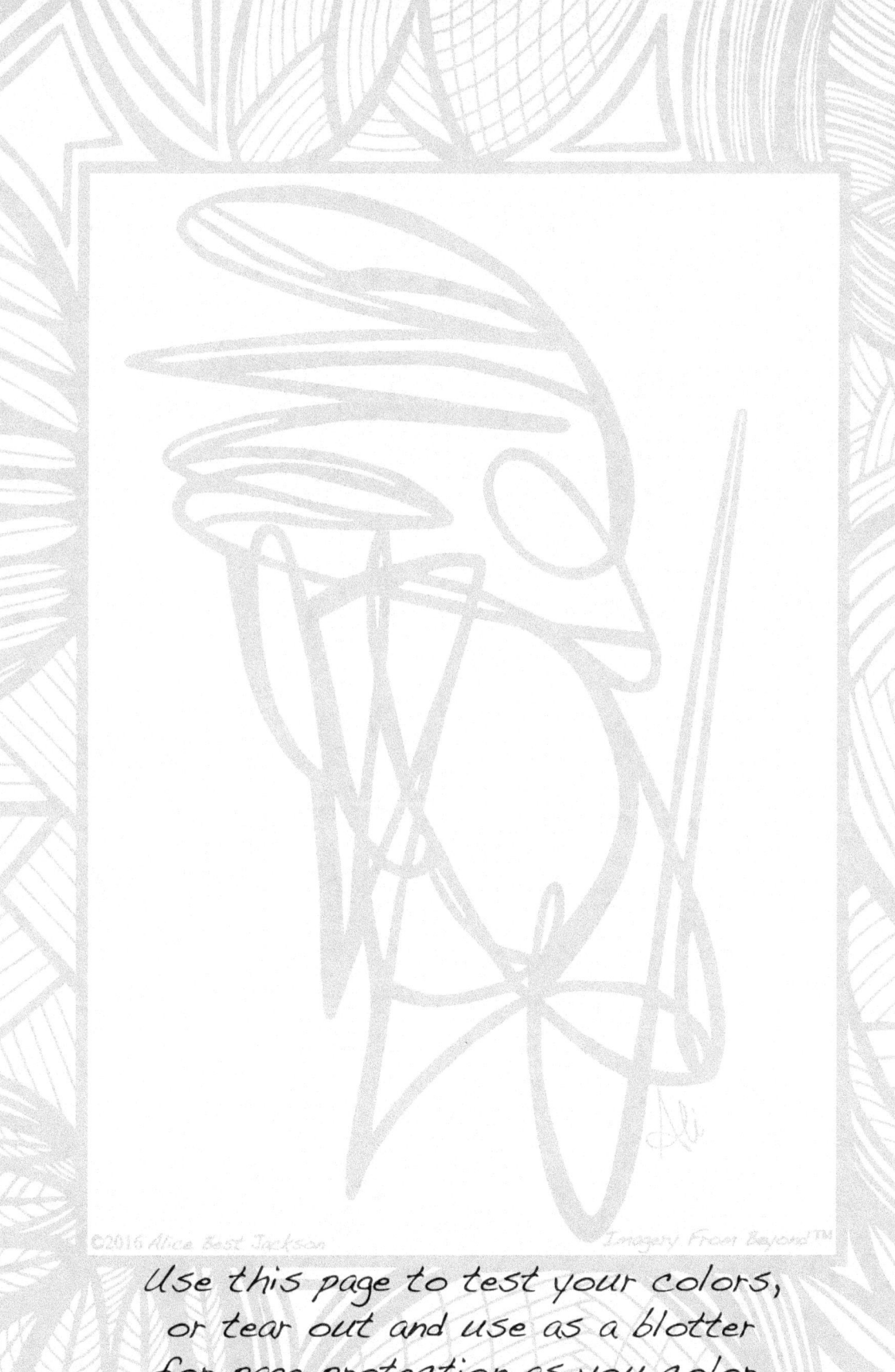

Imagery From Beyond™

Use this page to test your colors,
or tear out and use as a blotter
for page protection as you color.

www.ingramcontent.com/pod-product-compliance
Lightning Source LLC
Chambersburg PA
CBHW080703190526
45169CB00006B/2218